COLORADO
RASCALS,
SCOUNDRELS,
AND NO GOODS
OF BRECKENRIDGE, FRISCO, DILLON, KEYSTONE, AND SILVERTHORNE

COLORADO
RASCALS,
SCOUNDRELS,
AND NO GOODS

OF BRECKENRIDGE, FRISCO, DILLON, KEYSTONE, AND SILVERTHORNE

Mary Ellen Gilliland

Alpenrose
Press

ISBN: 1-889385-08-5

Library of Congress Control Number: 2005921789

Alpenrose
Press
Box 499
Silverthorne, Colorado 80498
(970) 468-6273
www.alpenrosepress.com
email: zoebooks@cs.com

Visit Our New Web Site!
www.alpenrosepress.com
More history!
Great old-time photos. Find also Mary Ellen Gilliland's hiking guides.
Directions for featured "Trail of the Week."
Hiking, ski and high altitude tips. Hikes into history. And more.

Alpenrose Press

Celebrating its 25th anniversary in 2005, Alpenrose Press of Silverthorne, Colorado has published more than 20 books on Colorado history, hiking and the outdoors.

The company began with Mary Ellen Gilliland's *SUMMIT, A Gold Rush History of Summit County, Colorado* in 1980. This lively history met with immediate success and has gone on to reprint several times and sell tens of thousands of copies. The book has received excellent critical review by well-known Colorado historians.

The Summit Hiker followed in 1983 and now, in its seventh revised edition, ranks as the area's best-selling book in several local bookstores. The historic hiking guide undergoes major revision every few years. In 1992 the guidebook became *The New Summit Hiker,* expanded from its original 40 trails to 50. The book also provides readers with 22 trails for ski touring and snowshoeing.

Gilliland's *The Vail Hiker,* a companion to *The Summit Hiker,* appeared in 1988. This title outsells every Vail Valley book. In 2001, it increased from 40 to 50 trails. Winter recreationists use its 30 ski and snowshoe routes.

Gilliland has also authored *Breckenridge! A Guide to Its Ghost Towns; Frisco, A Colorful Colorado Community*: and *Lula,* the story of a pioneer Keystone family; and now, *Rascals, Scoundrels and No Goods.*

CONTENTS

ACKNOWLEDGMENTS

This book's single biggest source of help came from my husband, Larry Gilliland, who provided information, photo scanning and practical support in a multitude of ways. Thank you, Larry!

Breckenridge historian Maureen Nicholls poured over the manuscript using her comprehensive historical knowledge to help with accuracy. Journalist and daughter Sheliah Gilliland lent editorial guidance. Summit Historical Society archivist Ann Rutledge gave research assistance. Summit County Library Director Joyce Dierauer helped with online historical newspaper research. Max and Edna Dercum contributed newspaper articles on James H. Myers. Long-time resident Sena Valaer provided stories about Dillon.

Obtaining photographs for a history as specific as this proved challenging. On hand to help meet that challenge were Summit Historical Society Dillon program coordinator Liz Duxbury; Frisco Historical Society museum administrator, Rita Bartram and her able assistant Sheryl Kutter; Ken Fiester; and Denver's Jane Cooper. Paulette Livers used her gift for graphic design to create the book's cover and interior art.

My warmest thanks to these wonderful helpers.

—Mary Ellen Gilliland

One: *A Parade of Saints and Sinners (Mostly Sinners)*

*W*arning: Should you decide to read this book, prepare your delicate sensibilities to be assaulted by escapades of charlatans, swindlers, seducers, rogues and imposters. Readers of noble character will find themselves forced to endure stories of depravity enacted by characters ranging from scamps to hooligans and may lament that their heretofore pristine souls are tainted by tales of the misdeeds of these reprobates. A Victorian lady would rush for her smelling salts at the first whiff of scandal—and so may you.

On the other hand, if the reader is one to relish the salacious (and the delicious), prepare for a smorgasbord of sin, a feast of felony, ranging from unsavory appetizer tidbits to a mulligan stew of misconduct, malfeasance and misdemeanor.

This book is a spoof of the straight-laced Victorians who preached morality and overlooked wildly illicit behavior, despite their sanctimonious society. The lawless mine camps of the West allowed those who escaped the restraints of Eastern and European society to

Victorian demands on women dominated even the primitive Ten Mile Canyon mine camps. This proper lady endures a stifling corset, a dangerous side saddle and a heavy, cumbersome hat. The camp's dirt roads muddy her skirt. Dress restraints were ludicrous.

taste freedom. The book's language mimics the pretentious verbiage of the era, as ornate and overdone as a Victorian parlor's décor. Words like reprobate, rake and blackguard described male wrong-doers. Strumpet, trollop and baggage designated fallen women. (For an amusing glossary of these terms, see page 184.)

The parade of saints and sinners that marched across the Summit County, Colorado gold rush scene included regrettably few saints. Instead, the frenzied scramble over the Continental Divide to places like Breckenridge, Parkville, Lincoln City, Frisco, Dillon and Montezuma invited a disruptive element. On the heels of the prospector came the claim jumper. Behind him sashayed the shyster lawyer, the gambler, shady lady, dishonest Injun, gunfighter, bootlegger, swindler, charlatan and cad.

While most of this book's stories depict lightweight criminals, they uncover—even among prominent upstanding citizens—a range of moral failures from the delinquent and debaucher to the deadly. All are real people who punctuated the history of gold- and silver-rich Summit County.

"Mornin'. The name's John Smith."

In fairness to the crooks and miscreants, an objective observer must admit that the environment of 1860s-1910s mine camps failed to nurture good behavior. Disappointingly, the gold rush drew escapees from civilized society. In July, 1860 when a post office opened in the nearby South Park town of Hamilton, 356 newcomers recorded their names as Smith, often John Smith. Those sending mail had to be specific in identifying the addressee. Cross-eyed John Smith, little John Smith or pot-gutted John Smith were nicknames that helped miners get their mail.

In Breckenridge 200 similar prospectors arrived daily in summer 1860. They were all male and formed an unruly bunch of non-acquaintances untamed by the presence of women. Primitive living conditions, lots of liquor and heinous sanitary conditions added to the rough nature of the tent, shanty and log cabin Breckenridge community. One prospector named Parsons came west in February and reported taking his first bath a full16 months later on a warm June day.

Even the western mine camp's main street offers a picture of the prevailing mayhem. Breckenridge had cellar-sized holes and mine shacks in its rubble rock Main Street. Some towns had worse. According to Vardis Fisher and Opal Holmes in their book *Gold Rushes and Mine Camps of the Early American West,*

In many places knee deep in mud . . . (the street was) plentifully strewed with old boots, hats, and shirts, old sardine boxes, empty tins of preserved oysters, empty bottles, worn out pots and kettles, old ham bones, broken picks and shovels, and other rubbish to various to particularize. Here and there, in the middle of the street, was a square hole about six feet deep, in which one miner was digging while the other was bailing water out with a bucket, and a third, sitting alongside the heap of dirt which had been dug up, was washing it in a rocker.

"A motley group of rough individuals" . . . 1860s author Bayard Taylor

Men from every field of labor came to the Rocky Mountain gold camps. Farmers, merchants, bankers, preachers, lumbermen, sailors and saloon-keepers came. Men of every nationality traveled to the American West, including Swedes, Norwegians, Britains, Scots, Welsh, German, Russian, Polish, Swiss and Chinese. Every color, white, yellow, red and black (such as Breckenridge black pioneer Barney L. Ford), came. These prospectors dressed in slouch hats and high boots with pants tucked into the boot tops, a loose and careless attire that a city gentleman would scorn. Women arrived later, both prostitutes in dancehall silks and strong steadfast women in calico who taught school, cooked for miners and raised children.

With this prospector influx came every kind of dancing and unholy music, frivolities that drew the fire-and-brimstone ire of Summit County's only real saint, Fr. John Lewis Dyer. The Methodist itinerant evangelist negotiated the high mountain passes on snow shoes, an early term for heavy wooden skis, to bring the gospel to the high altitude mine camps. In his book *Snow Shoe Itinerant,* Fr. Dyer said,

People of all classes came across the range, and of course, the inevitable dance house, with degraded women, fiddles, bugles and many sorts of music came too. There was a general hubbub from dark to daylight. The weary could hardly rest.

Young Howard Giberson, a short man, towers over pint-size powerhouse Jane Thomas, who broke up Frisco saloon brawls.

While some worked in the 1860s placer diggings as day laborers and others toiled on their own claims, many found themselves indisposed to the back-wrenching boulder-hoisting work of placer mining. These drifters, vagrants and truants lounged in saloons or chatted on street corners looking for trouble. And they usually found it.

"Almost every day was enlivened by its little shooting match. When the gambling saloon was crowded with people, drunken ruffians sometimes fired five or six shots from their revolvers, frightening everybody pell mell out of the room but seldom wounding anyone," one observer noted. This saloon report finds confirmation in the experiences of two local women. Breckenridge's Agnes Silverthorn described tavern shoot-'em-ups in *The Story of a Colorado Pioneer* by Evelyn Bradley. In a Frisco saloon, tiny Jane Thomas, less than five feet tall, often broke up fights, including a bloody knife brawl between two rowdies intent on slashing each other to death.

The continuous influx of newcomers fostered a community of strangers who shared one point of agreement: There are no rules above 10,000 feet. Night became day as construction workers hammered past midnight in the giddy rush to build towns, gun fights erupted with alarming frequency in late night saloon disruptions, dance halls poured piano music from their doors, drunks shouted in the street, burros brayed, horses neighed and sleepless babies wailed.

A group of eastern undergraduates, a bit too full of themselves, reeled in disgust after a visit to early Breckenridge. The trip notes from the 1877 Princeton Scientific Expedition to the Colorado mountains express the level of their loathing:

> To get out of the reach of the noise was impossible, and you might think that there was a den of wild animals being fed, or something worse. We heartily recommend Breckenridge as being the most fiendish place we ever wish to see. We were forced to spend the morning and the afternoon in the company of men whose language was vile and whose actions were tinged with a shade of crime that shocked and hurt our senses; never did anything so bestial and so unworthy even a mention by manly lips happen before our eyes.

The young men experiencing their undergraduate romp through the Rockies saw themselves as worthy of the early-day accolade "paragons of virtue." They considered themselves the capital fellows, the salt of the earth, the gentlemen and scholars of their generation. These, of course, were terms used to praise the righteous. A dictionary search for these noble titles yields precious little—less than a dozen. But a casual search for synonyms for "rascal" or "scoundrel" dumped out over 100 damning labels.

Whatever we call this book's eccentrics and however we describe their unsavory practices, they exhibit a woeful collection of human foibles, breaches of character and lapses of integrity.

To honor the best of Victorian-era etiquette, we begin with "ladies first." The ladies in this case are prostitutes—trollops, strumpets and chippies. Up front in their gaudy low-cut dresses, they lead a parade of liars and humbugs, charlatans and sneaks, rotters and scalawags, lechers, churls, hoodlums and knaves.

Please pass the smelling salts.

If you can "stummick " their misdeeds, as an old yarn-spinner would say, then reader, read on!

Two: *Shady Ladies*

The false front, hallmark of Victorian architecture, is amusing because it typifies the pretension of the late Victorian era, 1870-1901. Merchants and businessmen erected false fronts on their buildings to make the structures impressive. Victorian society similarly put up a false front of moral virtue. No where was this more apparent than in their contrivances regarding sexual immorality.

Victorians upheld rigid rules of sexual propriety. Adultery created a scandal. Despite strict laws regulating vice, every town had its cribs, parlor houses and saloon dance halls where each strata of male society—mine laborers, merchants and mining magnates—could buy sexual favors.

Victorian consciences remained clear for two well-rationalized reasons. First, ordinances confined prostitution to a certain area, the red light district. That equaled a firm stand against debauchery. Second, their town fathers licensed prostitution. That meant they could look their mothers in the eye. When money flowed into the town coffers from the madam's monthly $5 or $10 fee, and aura of righteousness and order prevailed. (Never mind the police magistrate, who had to knock red-faced on the parlor house door, to collect.)

Tough laws, laid down in strong language, satisfied the Victorian soul. A typical prostitution ordinance defined the lewd offender and identified the den of wickedness. In 1890 Breckenridge overhauled its laws and *The Summit County Leader* on February 5 published this:

BAWDY HOUSES

Inmates of Bawdy Houses – Patrons – Within Three Miles

Sec 12 Whoever shall keep or maintain, or shall be an inmate of any bawdy house, or house of ill fame, or place for the practice of prostitution or lewdness, or whoever frequents or in any way patronizes the same, or lets any house, room or other premises for such purposes, or shall keep a common, ill-governed and disorderly house to the encouragement of idleness, gaming, drinking, fornication or adultery, or other misbehavior within the town, or within three miles from the limits thereof, shall be deemed guilty of a misdemeanor and, upon conviction, be fined a sum of not less than five dollars nor more than two hundred dollars.

That these laws were widely ignored failed to trouble the Victorians. Defining and containing sin sufficed. In their towns both the church door and the saloon door swung wide. They allowed the family parlor and the parlor house, the preacher and the prostitute to coexist. If they zoned it, licensed it, fined it and frowned on it, vice was quite nobly contained.

This is why, despite Montezuma's strict vice laws, I can tell you the story of the town's longtime red light lady, Dixie.

Dixie, Soiled Dove

Montezuma, an 800-strong town in 1880, had its main street lined with hotels, restaurants, saloons, a general store, blacksmith shop, livery stable, mine offices, a meat packing plant and even a candy store. (That's civilized!)

The town flourished when 11,541 foot Webster Pass over the Continental Divide provided a vital connection to South Park and Denver in 1878. A year later, William Austin Hamilton Loveland built his skyscraping Loveland Pass road, nearly 12,000 feet at the Divide. On this new route ore freight rumbled out of mountain-barricaded Montezuma to Denver markets. Stagecoaches and freighters brought in passengers and supplies like good whiskey and the 1800s gourmet favorite, canned oysters. Miners, merchants and madams all cried, "Hurrah!"

The Snake River city incorporated in September, 1881 and immediately cracked down on crime. Montezuma's sporting element now winced as drunks forked over steep $5 to $25 fines, based on degree of dissipation. Gamblers paid $5 to $20 for indulging in popular pastimes such as faro, keno, shuffleboard, bagatelle or playing cards with intent to gamble.

Degraded women scurried from the law's glaring new language: "No bawdy house, disorderly house, house or ill-fame or assignation, or place known as a dance house shall be kept or maintained within the limits of Montezuma." Fines, ranging from $5 to a startling $50, exceeded those of drunks and gamblers.

All this legal posturing failed to faze Montezuma's resident red light lady, Dixie, who kept a neat white cottage back from Main Street. (Her home still stands on the right as you enter Montezuma.)

When Montezuma rode high on the price of silver, Dixie (real name: Ada Smith) employed several of what the Victorians called "frail sisters." When the Silver Panic of 1893 brought economic disaster, Montezuma's soiled dove flew solo.

In an era when proper ladies dressed in subdued gray, brown and black, Dixie sported huge picture hats with gaudy orange and fuchsia scarves.

As loud as her scarves were Dixie's cheers at local ball games. The town madam loved baseball. Each local town did also, fiercely supporting their own teams. Dixie seated herself in the stands, probably planning to zipper her lip. But when the competition intensified, a stream of blistering language disparaging the opposing team blared from her mouth. The proper matrons had to remove their children from the stands and seat themselves on rocks near the playing field.

Unlike Denver's voluptuous Mattie Silks, Montezuma's madam resembled a skinny old maid. Elizabeth Rice Roller in her *Memoirs from Montezuma, Chihuahua and Sts. John,* remembered seeing Dixie often as the madam shopped in the Rice family store. (Elizabeth was shushed into the back room when Dixie came in.) "She was known to all as 'Dixie' but Ada Smith was not glamorous. I can't recall that she was, in our times, ever even good looking—a little bit of a woman with a wrinkled face like a dried up apple."

Though Dixie had a bony body she possessed a soft heart. "She bought Columbine tinned milk by the case and fed it to the town dogs and cats," Elizabeth wrote. She loved coupons and deals, and also purchased huge jars of beef extract because the label offered a premium and because she used it to sustain Montezuma's dog population.

Her soft heart extended to former patrons when the prospectors, often disabled by hard work and mine accidents, grew feeble. Dixie carried soup to their cabins and nursed them through illnesses, possibly including the 1918 influenza epidemic.

She maintained "a certain dignity," according to Roller, and "kept her girls in line, insisting that they conduct themselves quietly to avoid the ill will of the community."

A Sham Artist

Sidestepping ill will was not the strong suit of a hussy in lamb's clothing who alighted from the Montezuma stagecoach on a blithe summer evening and managed to fleece the town flock.

Rosie had inquired of the stage driver about Mrs. Bianci, a kind Montezuma woman who had sheltered Rosie and her siblings after their mother died. Now married to a husband ill for many months, she found herself destitute with six small children at home. Once more, she needed help.

Mrs. Bianci had died, but her daughter, Isabella Black, remembered some pathetic dark-eyed children who had once shared their home. Touched she rallied the townsfolk to help Rosie. Donations poured in. Mrs. Black fed and housed young Rosie.

The town hosted a Friday night benefit for Rosie's children according to Elizabeth Rice Roller in *Memoirs from Montezuma, Chihuahua and Sts. John*. She herself sang a hit song of the day, "When I Lost You," while party-going miners tossed her their silver dollars. Next day, donors suggested that residents of nearby Sts. John might also contribute. Rosie trudged up the track to Sts. John and at sundown had not yet returned for her supper at Mrs. Black's.

Finally she strutted down Glacier Mountain on the arm of the Sts. John mine manager, known for his courtly ways but also his dissipation. Ignoring the shocked townspeople, they headed straight for the saloon. Hours later, the pair emerged. Most of the town's inhabitants, Rosie's benefactors, steamed with rage as the couple disappeared into Dixie's establishment.

Montezuma townsfolk, shown here in an 1890s photograph on the town grocery-post office porch, united to raise cash for a needy "Rosie." The sweet-faced waif turned out to be a con artist.

When Rosie and her paramour stepped from the parlour house on Sunday morning, she was unceremoniously escorted out of town. For months following, Montezuma citizens chafed when they heard Rosie's hit song. They renamed it, "When I Lost My Dough."

Montezuma had other red light ladies but Dixie outlasted them all, riding the boom-bust cycle of the mine town with aplomb. Her discreet behavior stood in sharp contrast to the flagrant invasion of Breckenridge by local strumpets in 1909, just four years after the police magistrate had run all the floozies out of town. With high hilarity, the ladies of the night, decked out in Merry Widow hats, feather boas and bare shoulders, took a wild ride up and down Breckenridge streets in a fancy hired rig. After stopping in the saloons for fresh courage, they descended upon the stores to shop. Respectable shoppers fled, according to Mark Fiester in *Blasted, Beloved Breckenridge*. The spree ended when the sheriff showed up with some strong-armed aides and returned the ladies to their proper domain.

HURDY GURDY HOUSES

In Breckenridge houses of ill repute flourished alongside dance halls. Both the fire-and brimstone-preacher, Fr. John Lewis Dyer, and pioneer Agnes Ralston Silverthorn complained about the dance halls. He lamented the vice; she could not stand the noise. Both had something to groan about.

Dance halls, called hurdy gurdy houses, blared raucous music into resident eardrums day and night. The hurdy gurdy, a hand organ with strings, keys and wooden wheels, produced music when the handle was turned. First played in Europe, it became a popular musical instrument in 1800s America. The girls who worked as dancing partners for the prospectors in 1860s Breckenridge were called hurdy girls or hurdies.

All spangles and smiles, the hurdy girl danced to hurdy gurdy music in mine camp dance halls. She made better wages than most miners.

These girls worked in halls where a bar occupied one side and a dance floor the other. A hallway with several small rooms, available to revelers wanting more than a dance, opened to the rear. Not all dance hall girls engaged in vice. The dance hall offered a good money-making opportunity to a pretty woman who did not want to degrade herself in prostitution. The male sporting element understood that while the dance was free, they were required to buy both themselves and their partners a $1 drink after each dance. Of the $1, the girl got half as her commission. The hurdies usually drank cold tea to insure their dancing agility. A popular hurdy girl could dance with 50 men in one evening, earning at least $50, and she got $25—a fortune in an era when mine laborers, working hard, earned $2.50 per day. The dance hall girls, known by their names and respected more than trollops, received admiration and friendship from their often-lonely male dance partners. In 1860s Breckenridge, the hurdy girl might be the only female a prospector saw all season.

This male comfort failed to cheer Fr. Dyer who despaired of "the general hubbub from dark to daylight." He opposed music and dancing, and scolded "the inevitable dance house, with degraded women, fiddles, bugles and many sorts of music."

Nor did it encourage Agnes Silverthorne who later told her granddaughter about the legendary racket.

Along with dance hall girls, Breckenridge had a lively assortment of fancy women, courtesans, strumpets, whores, harlots, hussies and madams. (Later you will read about a few of the Victorian matrons who could join this crew.) The stories of most fallen women are lost but tales of the Breckenridge madams still linger.

May Nicholson

After 1910 when gold began to play out, Summit County miners either left or homesteaded ranches along the Blue River north of Silverthorne.

Where did Breckenridge's current madam go? She followed the homesteaders down the Blue and became a cowgirl. Even cowgirls need to eat, so she started her own milk business, the Mayfair Guernsey Dairy.

May Nicholson, early Breckenridge's most colorful madam, witnessed a decline in clientele at her house of ill repute, The Blue Goose. Undaunted by the end of an era, she marched into the local bank and demanded her considerable savings. This she plunked down to purchase a ranch just below old Judge Silverthorn's Blue River placer claim, the core of today's town of Silverthorne.

Now those rolling green hills along the river are golf fairways, part of The Raven golf course. May's dairy barn remains there as a quaint reminder of the past.

Denver's Thomas Cooper, in an interview with the author, explained that he was a young survey crew member when he first met May Nicholson on her ranch in 1935. She exuded the independent spirit of the western ranch woman.

"May was some sight," Cooper remembers. She sat slender on her horse, ramrod straight. Her hair was a

Tom Cooper guided May's dude ranch guests on fishing trips.

brilliant carrot red. If you looked closely, however, you could notice the white roots of hair next to her scalp. She wore glasses with silver frames. This was no spring chicken!" Cooper's wife, Jane, later specified May's hair color as "shock-orange."

A smart business woman, May went from milking traveling salesmen and errant husbands to producing and selling ranch milk. She delivered the milk to customers on nearby ranches and all the way to Breckenridge. Herding dairy cows and hoisting milk cans wasn't easy. "She worked like a dog," Cooper says.

> May kept her new dark blue Buick sedan in one of her old log barns. She regularly delivered milk from five-gallon cans stacked on the rear seat. Once I ran into a new ranch owner in the Gore who asked me what I knew about May.
>
> "I called her up and asked if she could deliver milk to my house," he said. "She told me, 'Sure, I'll be happy to add you to my route. But here's one thing you've got to know. I used to run a whore house in Breckenridge. If that means a damn thing to ya, just forget it!'"

May sold milk out of the Buick's back seat till 1942, when her age forced her to abandon the Breckenridge route. Her milk then sold only at the Breckenridge Grocery. Still ranching, she advertised two-month-old piglets for sale in the July 9, 1943 *Summit County Journal* for $12. In August that summer her husband, Rusty, came up from Paonia, Colorado to help the aging May with her haying.

A talented horsewoman, May took a lead spot in the Kingdom of Breckenridge's No Mans Land parade, "either alone on her pacing horse or in the carriage of honor," Cooper recalls. Even in her elderly years when she had to move back to Breckenridge, May continued to

May Nicholson changed career horses in midstream. The Breckenridge whorehouse owner became a cowgirl. She trotted out her silver saddle and western costume to lead No Mans Land parade.

train horses. "She has a teeter-totter in her back yard and around age 80 still taught the horses to do tricks on it," Cooper says.

May's last Breckenridge home stood on Ridge Street. Moved decades ago, the building now houses Main Street's Prudential-Timberhill Real Estate.

As a horsewoman in her earlier days, May would have been a natural to guide the 1930s male tourist who took her dude ranch horse trips to the Willow Lakes high in the Gore Range. But she needed someone else to do the job. "She swore too much," Cooper lamented. Her raw language ran off even the toughest male guests. Because the Gore at that time was wild and untraveled, she needed a guide who knew the wilderness.

A teenager back in 1935, Tom Cooper fit the bill. He explained:

In 1935 my summer job on a surveying crew in the Gore Range involved running survey lines into May's ranch, so I looked her up for permission. My two summers on the survey job created in me a love for the Gore Range that lasts to this day. I'll bet even now I can lead you to unknown lakes still filled with large trout and to lost mines that may still be rich in gold and silver ore.

That knowledge led to a summer job with May. She had about a dozen good trail horses. Was I wrangler enough to take parties of dudes up to the Willows? After some coaching on the finer points, May let me loose overnight with about six of her dude guests. We made it but I insisted that everyone walk his horse through the steep and narrow parts of the high trails.

When young Tom planned to marry his sweetheart, Jane, he brought her to meet May. She signaled him an enthusiastic "thumbs up." He remembers being pleased.

"I thought a great deal of May because she was honest and sensitive," Cooper says. She was a real lady."

"She was a real tough lady," his wife Jane added.

Minnie Cowell and More Trollops

"Location, location, location." Breckenridge madam Minnie Cowell knew the businessman's mantra well. That's why she located her bawdy house on the heavily-used road to the Wellington and its busy mine neighbors in French Gulch. Minnie earned plenty of money but the courtesan did not keep it for herself. When a local family with a half-dozen children lost their home in a tragic fire, Minnie used her sin-gotten gain to buy the homeless family a new house.

Madams like Minnie and her competition, Madam de Webster and Alice Perry, encountered tough times when town governments decided to clean up their social stigmas. The *Breckenridge Bulletin* on Saturday May 27, 1905 smugly assumed that the clean up would last:

> Every feminine resident of the re-light district has accepted terms of the court to seek new fields and pastures greener not later than May 20. Some went to Alma, some to Denver and one or two to Goldfield.

Like a boomerang, the ladies returned.

Frisco's Fancy Women

The names of Frisco's madams remain a mystery. We do know that Frisco licensed prostitution. The town's license laws read: "All female, frequenters and inmates of dance halls, saloons and any house known to be kept for the purpose of assignations, (must pay) the sum of $5 per month." One imagines that the marshal got an eyeful when he made his monthly visit to collect the $5 license fee. He had to make the collection, however, because the $5 was applied to his monthly salary.

Because Frisco began as a planned community, launched by sober and enterprising capitalists, the town probably never had the cribs that lined the outskirts of the typical bawdy mine camp. The cribs, mere shacks that stood in a sordid line, housed the very young and less attractive trollops. The crib girls charged 25 cents to $2 depending on their age, attractiveness and experience.

Early Frisco attracted strong, stalwart characters probably untainted by lusts of the flesh. But in later years, when individual miners working their claims gave way to mining companies with their labor crews and management employees, parlor houses probably sprang up. Prostitutes there charged $1. Saloons, where assignations often occurred, flourished in early Frisco. A saloon or dance hall harlot made a fee plus a profit on the beer sold and possibly a tip.

Mine camp prostitutes never earned the money their city sisters got. But they received personal attention, often hearing themselves called by name. Sometimes they traded in their strumpet's clothing for a calico dress when they married one of their customers.

Kokomo Camp Followers

Kokomo in the upper Ten Mile Canyon lent a Parisian glitter to its dens of sin with three concert saloons and dance halls with the *faux* French names of The Light Fantastique, The Jardin Mabille and The Variety Theatre Comique. A fourth bordello chose a straight name, The Red Light Dance Hall. The Red Light had moved its girls to Kokomo from bawdy Leadville.

The nearby town of Robinson, which shamed Kokomo by having more saloons (24), also had dance hall girls who doubled as prostitutes. Two of these, Lillie and Mabel, made a suicide pact after Lillie's boyfriend, Thomas Lynch, beat her up. According to Stanley Dempsey and James Fell in *Mining the Summit,* the two swallowed a lethal potion and fell asleep locked in an embrace. The story has echoes of Romeo and Juliet. A friend came in and saved the life of a heavily-drugged Mabel, while Lillie, who took a larger dose of poisons, lay dead. The sordid life of the mine camp prostitute proved tragic.

THREE: *Thieves and Robbers*

laim jumping ran rampant from 1859 to 1862, the triple-crown years of Summit County's placer gold rush. Not only did thieves and ruffians seize and occupy a miner's diggings, they also jumped town residents' houses. Breckenridge stole the county seat from Parkville by snatching government records. Whole mining districts changed governance when bands of brigands jumped the region. Claim jumping reached its climax in a Ten Year War that bathed French Gulch in blood when gun battles erupted over the attempt to raid a Farncomb Hill wire gold nugget patch.

Claim Jumpers

All this marauding and plundering took place in the frenzy of the gold and silver rush. After spending their fortunes outfitting for Colorado, then transporting all their food, equipment, bedding, cookware and tools across the Great American Desert, the argonauts were seized by a greed-driven mania that defies description. Some expected to fill their gunnysacks with gold nuggets within days and return home to being rich as a full-time occupation. Others discovered that placer mining, digging in rock and boulder locked streambeds for free gold, was hard labor, an activity they loathed. Whatever the avarice-related motive, many prospectors yielded to the obsession of claim jumping. Gangs of thugs formed to overpower and seize other miner's claims. Claim jumping became as common as drunkenness or gambling.

Frenzied jumpers would swarm over a property when its prospector owner went to dinner. Brazen thieves sent notices illustrated with a rough-drawn death's head to claimholders or lot owners threatening assassination if the owner declined to vacate. Sometimes the jumpers didn't want the claim (too much work); they wanted to be bought off. Nevertheless, shootings, stabbings and murders punctuated these conflicts which numbered "without limit." According to eyewitness Daniel Ellis Conner in his *A Confederate in the Colorado Goldfields*:

> A miner could hardly leave his pit long enough to get his dinner without finding someone in it at work with all the tools left there when he returned. This was called jumping claims. The result of this sort of conduct was that neighboring claim holders united their protests on such occasions by visiting the "jumped" claim in an armed body and invited the intruder to leave, without standing upon the manner of going. This gradually got up a fashion of prepared resistance, again resulting unfavorable to mine owners. Lives were lost and conflicts inaugurated without limit.

Even mining districts, such as the extensive Montezuma mining district or the Blue River diggings, could be shanghaied by jumpers and its laws rewritten to satisfy the newcomers. Conner describes this:

A body of tramps would unite and "jump" the whole district, drive out the original owners and pass new laws, and work until they would be served the same way. But somebody always had possession.

This ravenous desire to grab the gold boggled visiting journalist J. Ross Browne who reported in the January, 1861 *Harpers* magazine.

Nobody seems to own lots except by possession . . . Nobody had any money; yet everyone was a millionaire in silver claims. Nobody had any credit, yet everyone bought thousands of feet of glittering ore. Everything underground was silver and deeds and mortgages on top.

While the lawless commandeered prospector property in the gulches and along creeks, did the folks like the clothing merchant, county clerk or assayer live in quiet security within town limits? Hardly. A man building a new home could leave to visit the hardware store and return to find that bandits had confiscated his construction project. A property owner busy building a fence around his several town lots arrived one morning to find that a jumper had completed his own fence just inside the owner's enclosure. The author's gold rush history *SUMMIT* details a house jumping incident where mob psychology reigned:

The ne'er do wells and rogues that populated every camp had a heyday in old Kokomo where the illicit practice of claim jumping went one villainous step further. When lumber ran scarce and rascals were plentiful, scenes like this May 1880 house jumping occurred.

Prospectors longed for a restaurant-cooked meal but dared not leave their gold diggings. Claim jumpers grabbed their claims and tools. Note blackened face and dark goggles to offset spring sun.

A gang of enraged residents all armed to the teeth rode into town at breakneck speed and reaching the building demolished the door and took possession. Five hundred citizens joined them and tore the building in fragments and scattered it upon the streets. Public sentiment is so strong against jumpers that hanging is openly discussed.

Leadville Weekly Democrat, May 22, 1880

The grabby mindset that made jumpers so rabid wormed its way into local government. Breckenridge's 1862-to-present role as Summit County's seat of government resulted from sacking the county records from the gold-rich town of Parkville. Sacking is a literal term because the records traveled in a burlap sack, according to Agnes Finding Miner who chronicled the memories of her grandmother, Agnes Silverthorn.

Pioneer Agnes Silverthorn, wife of the judge of the miners court, was Summit County's first (legitimate) business woman. She ran the well-regarded Silverthorn Hotel on Breckenridge's Main Street. Her experiences are recorded by her granddaughter in Agnes Miner's "Founding and Early History of Breckenridge, Colorado." This upstanding matron played a role in "jumping" the original Summit County seat of government.

A moonlight heist of the county records from Parkville, the first county seat, had taken place. Or so imaginative writers of history describe it. Historians disagree on the record-raiders' method (moonlight or daylight?), and county commission papers fail to establish the illicit transfer. But the documents did end up hidden in a cabin on Breckenridge's Main Street. Parkville outrage settled down during this discreet period of concealment. Then the documents were brought out and moved to the Silverthorn Hotel.

Its proprietor, Agnes Silverthorn, thwarted a second sacking of the records when the county clerk from Parkville came to rescue them. Her granddaughter wrote:

> My grandmother noticed the county clerk busily packing his records in a burlap sack and when he had been called out for a while she hid the sack, and in so doing saved the county seat for Breckenridge.

An eyebrow raiser: Breckenridge planted its roots as the county seat with pillaging of its own. And the town's most respected pioneer mother, Agnes Silverthorn, carried off the caper.

In her defense, Parkville was waning, with most of its free gold already taken. In contrast, Breckenridge boomed. By the late 1880s Breckenridge had matured from a rough log 'n shanty mine camp to a prosperous gold town graced by Victorian-style architecture. But the primitive banditry of the old camp sometimes broke through the Victorian veneer. The besieged Methodist preacher, Fr. John Lewis Dyer, lamented the habit of bawdy revelers from the saloons pirating his church organ when they wanted dance music. His book, *Snow Shoe Itinerant,* describes one incident: "About dark one night I heard something in the church, and ran out. A wagon was backed up to the door, and the organ was almost loaded."

More than "almost loaded" were the church robbers from the saloon. Their whiskey-induced gaiety wilted under the verbal scalding Fr. Dyer gave them that night. They slunk off empty handed.

Heisting an organ intended for accompanying the old Sankey and Moody hymns to liven up the dance hall was mischief. But a blow-your-head-off battle to steal Harry Farncomb's rich French Gulch nugget patch was brutish. Though scarred, wounded and battle-fatigued, Farncomb managed to survive the ten-year siege and emerge a richer man for it.

Harry Farncomb came with the early prospector rush to the 1860s Blue River diggings. Shortly after his arrival Farncomb stumbled upon placer gold in French Gulch. Farncomb's unusual ore twisted in interlocked strands of pure, highest-quality crystallized gold. Searching on the hill above his placer discovery for the source of this eroding free gold, he found his stunning "wire patch," a hard rock deposit of rich, sculptured wire gold. Farncomb spent the next several months quietly purchasing property on the soon-to-be-famous hill.

The *Rocky Mountain Magazine,* published in Denver in 1908 looked back at Harry Farncomb's bonanza strike, his Wire Patch mine group and the maelstrom it created. The unnamed magazine author has surely embellished the story because it sounds like *Amazing Comics,* and he has probably erred in some facts. But it's good story so here it is:

> One day there appeared on the scene a young man, a mere boy in his teens . . . the boy, practical beyond his years, was peering with his mind's eye into the hill above where he calculated the greatest deposits of the shining yellow metal would be found. He calculated as geological minds have since calculated that the underlying wealth was worth hundreds of millions and that his calculations were worthy of respect is evidence by the $30,000,000 in gold already obtained and the vast areas that remain unopened. The hero of our story dug with the others and often obtained a pound a day which amounts to $820 and which designates the master miner . . . He secured 40 acres. He soon took out enough gold to employ a force of men and provide proper equipment to increase his operations which

proved extremely profitable and made him one of the big men of the camp.

But before the fortune came the battle that caused death, grief or ruin to many and often threatened the life of the young man who fearlessly defended his property. The trouble began, as the story is told by an old Breckenridge miner, when the young operator appeared in a bank in Denver with a sack of gold which was in chunks weighing from one-half to two and one-half pounds each, which he placed on deposit. The news flashed down the street and caused great excitement. The result was that a conspiracy was formed, to secure forcible possession of the property. The conspirators numbered sixteen.

. . . A man named Murphy, the leader of the gang and a man of great strength and courage, hid in the timber along the mountainside to block the return of the owner. They met alone and fought for about an hour unobserved. When the lad established his mastery over the bully, the faces of both were masses of red pulp and the fingers of the boy's left hand were almost severed by this opponent's teeth. Murphy left the camp in mortification . . .

The lad, knowing that he was in for another fight, and with unknown odds against him, trudged onto the mine. There he found fifteen men armed with guns. As he entered the door he was rushed upon by the leader. A blow with the butt of a six shooter put his man out of the fight and with a six shooter in either hand he waded into the crowd, scattering them right and left. Single-handed he not only put the gang to flight but saved $10,000 in gold which was on the plates of the mill. The gang was desperate, however, and returned after dark, firing a volley into the building where the lad and a few of his friends, who were quickly gotten together, were standing guard. The volley was quickly returned and from the number of shots the conspirators realized that assistance had been secured during their absence.

The desperadoes retreated to the safety of boulders and trees along the mountainside and then mounted a gun battle that lasted till 3 a.m. None of the 40 men fighting died but several from both sides received serious wounds.

The conspirators launched a legal battle that continued for ten years, 1877-87. The lawsuits cost a small fortune to mount. Every lawyer who landed in Breckenridge worked the case, representing the side that persuaded him first. The bank in Denver which funded the conspirators suspended their account due to the heavy withdrawals necessary to maintain the fight. In the meantime, Harry Farncomb lived in fear of his life:

> During the legal battle the youthful mine operator was murderously sought day and night and not one minute of the ten years' struggle was he left unguarded. A story is told of one man who tried for a year and a half to assassinate him and failing to get the drop on him put a bullet through the heart of one of his followers while the latter was drunk and asleep on a pool table.

While the bank ran dry for conspirators, Farncomb feverishly mined the rich Wire Patch for gold to pay legal and protection costs. The Wire Patch proved richer than any opposing cash source and Farncomb, who was in the right anyway, won the legal battle. The riches on his legendary hill include one pocket that yielded $163,000 worth of crystallized gold in four days, according the 1908 *Rocky Mountain Magazine*. (Think of $163,000 as big money in the 1880s when coffee cost 10 cents a pound and a nice house cost under $1,000.)

ANOTHER WAR, THIS ONE FOUGHT OVER SILVER

Harry Farncomb survived his Ten Years War. However, another menaced mine owner failed to survive the attempt to commandeer his silver mine, the rich Smuggler near the old town of Robinson. He was Colorado Lt. Governor-elect George Robinson, who won the office in the November 1880 vote. The town below Fremont Pass that bore his name had become a thriving hub of Summit County with mills, a smelter, hotels and its own newspaper, the *Robinson Tribune*. George Robinson's silver-laced Smuggler mine proved so rich that every avaricious schemer around wanted to grab it.

At the pinnacle of his career in 1880, Robinson became embroiled in a dispute with Captain J.W. Jacque (think Jacque's Pique, a ski run at Copper Mountain) and others over Smuggler ownership. Armed conflict threatened to erupt. Robinson placed rifle-bearing guards at the Smuggler and ordered them to fire on any intruders.

Alarmed by a warning that a 100-man gang would attempt to capture the mine on November 27, 1880 Robinson heard a second disturbing rumor. The guard at the tunnel's mouth had deserted his post in fear. Accompanied by mine manager J.C. Brown, Robinson went up to inspect the guard post. Behind the heavily bolted door the guard, Patrick Gillin, remained on duty.

"Don't go too close to that door, Mr. Robinson," warned Brown.

"I just want to see if everything is all right," responded Robinson, advancing along the narrow path to the tunnel opening. He reached the door and shook it to check its lock.

"What do you want?" Gillin cried out from inside.

Not hearing Robinson's reply Gillin immediately shot through the door. The bullet caught Robinson as he turned to leave. He suffered greatly from the wound for almost two days and died November 29.

He would have taken office in the State Capitol just weeks later.

Legend says that a dying Robinson rewarded Gillin with $1,000, the amount promised for killing the first intruder to threaten the disputed Smuggler. (He put the money in the bank. See the next section, Embezzlers and Crooks, to find out what happened to the cash.)

Readers, what do you think of these crooked, black-hearted claim jumpers? Maybe you share my conclusion: Among the vipers, snakes and bad eggs that poison the pages of this book, claim jumpers may be the most toxic.

Embezzlers and Crooks

Carbonateville, a short-lived neighbor to Kokomo in the upper Ten Mile Canyon below Fremont Pass, launched its history with larceny. An October 16, 1879 *Rocky Mountain News* article related the sticky-fingered story of Anthony Blum, a Carbonateville banker who embezzled bank funds and left bank customers holding the bag.

The Merchants and Miners Bank of Carbonateville opened in February, 1879 during the frenzied onset of the silver boom in the upper Ten Mile. Anthony Blum, president, partnered with A.H. Reynolds to start the $50,000-capitalized institution. Carbonateville had burst into being in 1878 on a plateau at the mouth of wildly-rich McNulty Gulch. Leadville miners had struck gold there in 1860. The gulch relinquished $3 million in free (placer) gold its first three seasons, a stunning amount when a dollar bought a fine dinner and night's hotel stay. Miners later abandoned McNulty Gulch. Then in

1878 hard rock silver discoveries spearheaded a second rush. Carbonateville exploded, quickly gaining 61 businesses, including six hotels, four grocers, seven saloons, two sawmills—and one bank.

The Merchants and Miners Bank enjoyed a brisk business in gold exchange, loans and customer accounts. Its president enjoyed community prestige. Then Anthony Blum yielded to temptation, writing himself handsome checks including a note for $800 "signed" by Mr. Boedecker and negotiated at the First National Bank of Leadville, according to Summit County's first newspaper, the Kokomo-based *Summit County Times.* The $800 note alerted a Leadville bank official who queried Blum. The forger wrote a flurry of additional checks to Denver and New York banks. His felonious spree took place on September 26, 1879 but Blum adroitly dated the checks September 29, giving himself time to abscond. He established a phony mailing address as J.J. Weicher at Leadville for forwarding of mail and express packages.

Then Blum went to Leadville to buy some time. He planned to stage a drama. On a visit to the First National Bank he met with bank official Mr. Ordean, who had spotted the fraudulent $800 note. Blum "struck a doleful keynote of penitential wailing, said he ought to shoot himself," the newspaper reported. He begged for time to make the $800 fraud good. The melodrama of Blum's tearful hand-wringing swayed Ordean to keep quiet.

Back in Carbonateville, a warrant for the bank president Blum's arrest was issued. The law shot a telegram to Denver authorities to request the embezzler's arrest upon arrival there. Telegraph lines had just been constructed. Felon's luck prevailed when the new lines immediately went down and the telegram never reached its destination. Blum padded his pockets with several thousand dollars in cash belonging to bank customers such as James Coffey, the Carbonateville meat market proprietor and Patrick Gillin, a miner (he lost $250, a considerable sum). The slippery Blum escaped, never to be found.

Dredge King Cleaned Out

Larceny, both grand and petty, plagued the early days of Colorado mountain camps. Human nature being subject to frailty and foibles, robberies continued after the gold and silver rush ended. Around 1918 Ben Stanley Revett, the gold dredge king, saw his lavish home, Swan's Nest, repeatedly looted by persistent burglars despite the efforts of a hired caretaker.

J.G. Collins, a family man and Revett neighbor, systematically pilfered Revett's possessions, allegedly using his own wife and family to purloin clothing, rugs, draperies, linens, lamps, guns and assorted belongings from Swan's Nest. He stripped the place. Instead of decorating his own home as a miniature replica of Swan's Nest, Collins stuffed the furnishings into an old house he used as a storeroom. And instead of enjoying a Merry Christmas in December, 1918 Collins found himself in the calaboose. With Collins convicted in April, 1919 according to a *Summit County Journal* news story, the Revetts heaved a sigh of relief about their Swan River summer home. The caretaker, Mrs. Melissa Hayden, let down her guard.

Just weeks later, a riled Mrs. Hayden, who had helped police located the loot filched by Collins, reported another ransacking. Between her two visits to Swan's Nest on April 27 and May 5, thieves raided a Revett cabin and broke the lock on the Swan's Nest door to steal two fine saddles. The normally-responsible Melissa Hayden, who also held positions as Summit County Schools Superintendent and Breckenridge postmistress, must have been embarrassed. Happily for Hayden and Revett, the safe at Swan's Nest was barricaded with successive layers of mine rail, steel plate and dredge rock.

Road agents hold up a stagecoach party and steal the cash passengers needed to stake a claim or start a business. If the gal were packing a pistol, she could change the crime's outcome.

JESSE JAMES UNWITTINGLY OUTWITTED

Tom Marshall, patriarch of a local ranch family from Acorn Creek north of Silverthorne, drove an early day stagecoach. On a particular run from Denver to Leadville via Buena Vista, he carried a valuable mine payroll. Two stagecoaches traveled together to thwart violence and robbery on bandit-infested 1860s and '70s post roads. That security measure unraveled when Tom Marshall's coach broke a wheel rim. During the time taken to repair it, the other coach contin-

Jesse James historians debate whether this ominous pair is really Jesse and Frank James. The pistol-fortified bravado of the young desperadoes typifies the western hooligan.

ued on. The James boys, aware the stagecoach carried the payroll, ambushed and held up the first stagecoach. The pistol-toting robbers came up empty handed. Puzzled, the highwaymen rode away. Tom Marshall rolled safely to Leadville with the payroll intact. History indeed records a brief and little known James gang foray into the Leadville area for the profitable purpose of holding up stagecoaches. Later as a lower Blue River rancher he loved to tell his grandchildren of the day Jesse James did not hold him up.

FOUR: *Swindlers and Cheats*

*T*he author believes that Montezuma town marshal tells *Gassy's tale better than anyone. So she has recreated his sorry tale through the persona of that inside observer.*

Gassy Thompson: A Swindler's Story

Halloo, folks! Sit down right here. I've got a queer tale to tell you.

I'm Theo Newman, town marshal here in Montezuma, also servin' the camps of Sts. John, Wild Irishman, Chihuahua and Keystone.

Here's my story: It wuz a reg'lar May afternoon, sleet and corn snow, grey as an undertaker's longjohns. I leaned back in my swivel chair here, feet restin' on my rolltop desk, when three gents bust through thet door. No hobnail boots and muck stained overalls like our silver minin' boys, no rumpled suit of store-bought clothes like our Montezuma merchants. No sir. Fine Eastern gentlemen, with oiled boots and derby hats. One of 'em's puffin' a good Havana, other sportin' a gold watch chain, third has a real red carnation in his breast pocket.

"What do you know about this scoundrel, Gassy Thompson?" the short one with the cigar demands.

"I can't claim to know much, yer honor," replies I. "Hear he's been hired out to bore a mine tunnel up the crick in Horseshoe Gulch."

"At *our* mine, the Peruvian," pipes up the one with the posy. "We've just come west to commence work there. We snowshoed in early this morning on the crust to get a tunnel crew started to work. Mine tunnel, humbug! That charlatan has cheated us!"

"Criminal!" one shouted. "Miscreant! Felon! Reprobate! Snake in the grass," they hollered, each voice louder than the first. They wuz buildin' up a head of steam like a preacher sermonizin' on hellfire.

"Whoa, gents," I said, bringin' my feet to the floor. "Back up and tell me what happened."

Well, folks, they told me thet this Gassy Thompson had 'cepted their contract to drive the Peruvian's new 100-foot tunnel just below the Continental Divide. Thet's the one at 12,000 feet up thet wind-blasted Horseshoe Basin. A camp called Peru with six or so cabins stood up there close by the new road Commodore Decatur had put over Argentine Pass. Them Easterners had greenbacks 'nuff to light their cigars with and they trusted their money to any feller who knew a pick axe from a shovel. And I must opine in his favor thet Gassy Thompson wuz the best drill striker in the territory.

Anyhow, Gassy hired a gang in November, promisin' the three Eastern investors a

Theodore Newman

good true tunnel by April. They could fill their pokes with silver by June when the snow melted. Pigs in clover, they'd be.

The task wuz a tough un. Borin' through thet stubborn Ruby Mountain granite with drill rods and blastin' powder was harder than bitin' into a brimstone biscuit baked up by the devil hisself. I guess old Gassy wasn't prone to sweat when he could use his connivin' powers instead.

When them heavy Horseshoe Basin snows begin to fall Gassy still had jest a little dirt outta the hole. He hatched an unholy plan. He begin buildin' thet tunnel backasswards, timberin' his square sets *outside* Ruby Mountain aginst its wall. Now thet basin gets snow up to a rich man's collar buttons in early winter but them big heavy snows, three shovel lengths deep or more, come in March and April. Hell, the snow don't melt till June up there. The winter and spring snow buried them square set timbers good, makin' a sham tunnel. A fake. It wuzn't no real tunnel, just a frame of wood timbers alongside the mountain.

The Philadelphia gents come in on the narrow gauge in April to eyeball Gassy's work. Bein' greenhorns as they wuz, they were plumb fooled and paid him off in silver dollars—with a bonus to boot. Thet scoundrel hopped the first narrow gauge train out of Keystone station, no more to be seen. He skeedaddled south to his hole in the San Juans. I had heard enough.

"I'll hev a look into this," I told the hornswaggled threesome, usherin' them to my door. "I doubt it'll do much good. Thet Gassy's no holy Methodist. But it takes a trio of greenhorns like you to give a born swindler his lifetime opportunity."

Their eyebrows shot up. I tipped my cap and shut the door.

Now a man don't need to tell everythin' he knows and what I didn't tell those Eastern gents is that I knew a lot more about Gassy Thompson than I let on. A lawman doesn't rightly want to mess with the likes of him. He kin knock a man like me off'n his high horse as easy as he hits a spittoon with a squirt of tobacky juice. He's damn good at schemin' and always has him an answer.

Fer instance, thet time in the fall of 1862 when Gassy was haulin' a load of logs he had cut to sell up at the Tenth Legion Mine near Georgetown. I just happen to know the two sourdoughs who were settin' down to supper in their cabin just below thet same mine road. They had cooked up some mighty fine vittles. Yep, roasted bighorn sheep and venison was piled up high on those tin plates and they wuz ready to man the trencher. Then they heard a loud crash. Immejitley a load of dirt, 'nuff to fill up an ore car, poured down from the roof of their cabin, which wuz made from brush an' sod. It dumped on them and ruined thet good dinner.

Madder 'n hornets the two come out of the cabin and there's Gassy, cool as a cucumber, askin' "What will you give me for thet load of firewood I jest delivered onto your cabin roof?"

I grant you thet I'm warmin' to my own yarn spinnin'. Let me give you some of this fine coneyack here—wal at least the jug says coney-ack on it, right 'ere, see. Nothin' like swallerin' down the good stuff to settle a man's stummick, especially if he's a bachelor cookin' for his-self. Probably the reason Gassy drew thet monicker—real name is George, y'know. Prob'ly cooked up his own beans like I do and didn't start 'em early enough. Sunday beans won't be tender up this high unless you start bilin' 'em Friday after breakfast. Wal, I was tellin' you about Gassy Thompson, not about cookin' beans.

Winter of 1874 Gassy took a work contract, as he was always doin' cuz he couldn't stand to work for no boss, to open a shaft thet some miners had abandoned sev'ral years back. Gassy goes up the crick to spy out the job and to his wonderin' eyes finds 125 feet of water in the shaft. Thar's a corker, for sure, cuz it would cost Gassy $1

Is this George "Gassy" Thompson? We're not entirely sure. The dress and attitude say, yes.

a foot to pump out the sump, thereby wipin' out his profit.

Next day Gassy coaxes a miserable mongrel dog to follow him up the snowy trail to the mine. When man and beast come upon the shaft, Gassy slits the dog's throat and slops blood around. It wuz just like them Old Testament brothers did with thet goat's blood to make Joseph look murdered. Gassy musta read his Bible because right 'ere wuz the same trick them rotten Israelite boys used. He tied a heavy stone to the misbegotten carcass of thet mutt and pitched him into the watery pit. Then he hightailed it back to the camp and told me, the marshal, thet a turrable crime had been committed. Boys, I was fooled somethin' awful when I saw all thet blood. I got them county commissioners to hev a meetin' and they put up the money for a crew to pump the water outta thet shaft to recover the *habeus corruptus.* Thet'd be Latin for them wot don't know. We got suspicious when we fished out thet dead dog. I got my comeuppance from Gassy Thompson thet day.

And wot did Gassy get thet day? He got his work done for nothin'.'

I can hear your mind concludin', *thet fellow ought to be hung.* And thet's what nearly happened. Up there on Kelso Mountain, Gassy worked alone hammerin' a single jack into some mule-stubborn ore.

Every few strikes with the hammer and the chisel, akshully a gad to be specific, would pop out and fall 20 feet below to the floor of the stope. Cussin' like a Cossack, Gassy would climb down and get thet confernal gad. Now Gassy had him a clever wit. But this day thet wit wasn't working its shift because he tied one end of a rope to the short drill and haltered the other around his neck to solve the harrassin' difficulty. Back at his hammerin' Gassy felt the stagin' give out and he fell like a hunk of lead carbonate—until the rope jerked tight on his neck. Wal, rascals is jest lucky by nature and some of the boys happened along. They saw Gassy with his neck nearly broken and the wind leavin' his bellows at a frightful rate. So they cut him down, doin' no favors to the gullible of the population, I might opine.

An thar's no man more gullible than the young minin' engineer fresh out of school with his ears still wet. One Peter Dean came west to Colorado to larn the practical arts of minin' and to get some sense knocked into his fool school head. At Leadville young Dean met none other than Gassy Thompson. A friendly saloonkeeper confided to the greenhorn thet Gassy knew minin' better than anyone.

Next day young Peter followed Gassy to the 50-foot shaft he and his partner Pot-gut Jim was workin'. While Jim manned the windlass which was rickety as hell Gassy and Peter Dean went down the shaft in the bucket. Gassy hit with the sledge hammer for starters while Peter turned the drill. When the hole was opened to Gassy's satisfaction, he stuffed it with dynamite and sent Peter up top. When Jim had the bucket up, they let it back down. Gassy lit the fuse and yelled "fire in the hole!" The two up top heaved to crank thet windlass. With Gassy up, they ran for cover. Minutes later a huge explosion about shattered Peter's eardrums.

Gassy repeated this work pattern several times before he squinted at the newcomer. "Looks like you wuz born to minin', son. I'm gonna let you have the next shot. Usual I just wouldn't feel justified allowin' a tenderfoot to fire a shot for plumb three months but you've got a genius for minin'. It comes to you easy as robbin' a bird's nest."

I'm not sayin' this compliment gave Peter a swolled head but it did strengthen his manliness. Down in the hole Peter finishes stuffin' dynamite into the rock and lights the fuse. "Hoist away," he hollers out. The bucket jerks up about 10 feet and stops dead. Peter can hear cussin'. An awful disagreement is goin' on up above. Peter is swingin' helpless as a kitten above the charge. The fuse is spillin' fire like forty fiends outta hell and the boys up top are usin' their fists. Whether from smoke or fear, the greenhorn passes out.

Later he comes to under a tree. He larns thet the whole damned thing was a joke. Gassy put no dynamite in the charges thet time.

Next mornin' Peter comes down for breakfast in the hotel and the boarders tell him his hair has turned white.

And Gassy's already at the bar tellin' the boys about how he initiated the tenderfoot. "It gives 'em nerve," he bragged to one and all. "Put's heart into 'em."

Wal, every yarn has its end and Gassy's tale ain't no different. After the bald-faced swindle he carried off at the Peruvian Mine near Montezuma, Gassy high-tailed it to the San Juans, which you will recall if thet coneyack didn't addle your brain bad enough to miss parts of a good story. Gassy Thompson upped and died there a few years later. The miners back then accorded even a cheatin' liar a decent burial. And he got one.

High Graders

Before we delve into the disreputable habit of pilfering gold dust, pocketing nuggets and purloining high-quality ore, let's take a language lesson. As a noun, high grade refers to rich ore, the best quality yield. High grade also can mean a rich piece of ore, like a gold nugget. As a verb, to "high grade" means to steal nuggets, flakes or dust from a mine

The Peruvian Mine, high in the wind-buffeted Horseshoe Basin on Peru Creek, witnessed one of Gassy's infamous swindles.

you don't own, either a placer gold claim or underground workings.

High grading hit Summit County, Colorado about the same time as white gloves, calling cards, champagne and wallpaper—the 1880s. The 1860s-70s placer miners mostly worked their own claims and had no reason to pilfer. But when the 1880s hardrock boom began, more mining companies organized, a step removed from the individual miner and a partner or two. By the 1890s, large corporations had consolidated prospector claims and mine company properties into large-scale operations, often owned by absentee Eastern investors. Mine employees found it easy to supplement their family incomes by filching a gold nugget here, pinching a sample of dust there. A small nugget could equal a week's wages. Most miners felt high grading compensated for the accident-prone, health-destroying work they did for about $3 per day. In fact, some believed they were entitled to steal.

One gold camp preacher, sermonizing on the sin of theft, added this disclaimer for the miners in his audience: "But gold belongs to him wot finds it first."

The community supported this misguided belief. Merchants in mining equipment and tools, grocery and general stores accepted high grade as easily as cash. Saloons took gold dust as payment for whiskey. Even the ladies of the night tucked a gold nugget into the bosom of their low-cut bodices as payment for services rendered.

Unlike cash, however, high grade could be traced to its source. Experienced assayers, geologists, mining engineers and some miners themselves could examine ore and tell you not only what mine produced it, but also what underground level and specific work area it came from.

No wonder high graders used home grinders to pulverize the stolen ore till it defied detection. No wonder they bribed unethical assayers who possessed both the skill and the right equipment to melt the booty down to gold bullion, an untraceable but highly valuable commodity.

Unsavory sharks and syndicates bought the plunder from high graders. Unscrupulous assayers purchased high grade. They sold it to the U.S. Mint in Denver which like the hurdy gurdy and hardware store asked no questions. Breckenridge's Farncomb Hill mining magnate John Campion reputedly paid a handsome price for ore pirated from his own mine.

Let's step into the hob nailed boots of the ordinary mine worker. If he whistled off to work on the hill carrying a tin lunch pail or sporting a tall and sturdy looking hat—watch out. He might be a high grader. Many stories of high-grading revolve around the Cornish miners, called the "Cousin Jacks" whose lunch pails often clanked with stolen ore on the way off the hill. Gold is heavy and the weight of those contraband-carrying lunch pails caused both bandy legs (bow legs) and hernias. Worse, stories of high-grading as early as the 17th century England and Wales caution that high graders would be banished from mine jobs and their houses burned.

When American mine owners wised up and searched tin lunch pails here, miners relied on hats with false crowns or a double hat which could hold up to five pounds of high grade. Even a hatband on a soft felt hat could hide stolen ore. The bounders also used a long sock or cloth tube suspended inside a trouser leg; pockets sewn into a waistband or the popular corset cover, a chemise of canvas with pockets like a fishing vest to hold stolen specimens. Hollow boot heels worked well. Lunch pails with false bottoms and even uneaten food hid the contraband ore even through a search. While his Cornish pastie may have gone uneaten to provide a vehicle for hidden treasure, the miner may have filled up on nuggets instead! Swallowing small nuggets was rare but inserting the nuggets into body cavities was not.

Ingenious miners created the tube mill, a short length of capped iron pipe with a piece of rod that worked as a pestle. The small tube, easy to hide behind rock in the mine, pulverized gold inserted into it with just a few strokes of the rod. Granular gold could not be traced to any individual mine. If the miner couldn't smuggle out the purloined gold on his body, he could hide it in a sack of debris headed for the outside.

To combat theft, mine owners installed changing rooms, sometimes with mandatory showers or bath vats because a smear of clay on a miner's body could hold a half teaspoon of dust, worth $10 in a day when a bushel of tomatoes cost 5 to 10 cents. Miners greased their hair and smeared gold dust into it. (Bar keepers in saloons did the same thing, often running their fingers through their pomaded hair after taking a prospector's dust in payment for a drink.) As high graders got smarter, mine owners got tougher. Strip searches and the demand that miners squat and lift a heavy object to evacuate gold hidden in body cavities before leaving the changing room outfoxed scheming miners. Also companies whose shift bosses tolerated high grading hired outside spies to watch the workers.

The pilferers retaliated by staging a work slowdown, a profit-wrecking practice that made mine owners endure theft as the lesser of two evils. Or miners avoided changing room scrutiny another way. They simply got the ore outside the mine without transporting it on their bodies. When low grade ore rolled out of the mine to be discarded on the dump, the ore car sometimes contained a stash of high grade. The embezzling worker returned at night with a lantern to retrieve his loot. Some brazen high graders invaded mines at night and worked, drilling and detonated small blasts of explosives that could not be heard above.

But who enjoys night work? Conniving scalawags could steal their employers blind in broad daylight.

At the ore mills high grading continued as a time-honored practice in a different form. Here workers with fertile minds found opportunity to filch from retort rooms, steal gold amalgam from the separators and lighten the load at the loading dock.

Actually the efforts companies made to thwart high grading ended up benefiting miners. Stove-heated changing rooms provided miners coming off a 12-hour shift a chance to get out of wet clothes, clean up and warm up before they braved a cold walk home at night. They reduced chances of the number one mine camp killer, pneumonia.

Avoiding cold, wet work was the very ruse one schemer used to carry off a lucrative heist. The champion high grader of Farncomb

Is this ore worth putting in my pocket? This question lurked in many mine workers' minds. High grading was a common practice.

Hill, who will remain anonymous, once visited some extremely rich ground above the French Gulch town of Lincoln. He lingered, despite a soaking rainstorm, and the placer claim's owner offered him $3— the going rate—to help with cleanup of some valuable ore-bearing dirt. The double dealer protested that it was raining too hard to work and the he wanted to avoid getting drenched. He offered to work for $2.50 per day the next morning. As the pair finished up the next day, the placer's owner, frustrated, complained about the small profit. The helper replied that he hated to accept the $2.50 daily wages but needed the cash. Turned out that the bounder had returned in the rain and worked all night with a lantern extracting the gold by himself. He had then showed up tired but happy to work the worthless tailings with the unsuspecting owner next morning.

Even more bold was the sneak who bragged around Breckenridge in his later years about the outrageous ore thefts he had carried off. He worked for Tom Groves, the discoverer of Tom's Baby, Colorado's largest gold nugget at a stunning13 pounds 7 ounces troy weight. Tom always led his employees out of the mine at day's end through a long tunnel. The crook noticed that Tom usually glanced at a certain set of timbers. So the high grader marked the set and slipped in by night to uncover a big cache of nuggets hidden there. He replaced the timbers in good order and Tom Groves never spoke a word about his loss.

The most daring act ever performed by this consummate high grader was to steal a red-hot retort from mining magnate Robert Foote, who owned a number of mines and Breckenridge's best lodgings, the Denver Hotel. A retort was a glass vessel with a long tube used under high heat to extract gold from accompanying ore. The vessel was in an oven in the mine's boardinghouse kitchen, its temperature made very hot after the cook had removed the food items. A guard on duty stepped away, sure than anyone who touched the retort would be identified by his tortured screams. But this dauntless felon grabbed the searing retort and stuffed it into his shirt. The cook, returning from dumping dishwater out the back door, saw the thief doubled over in pain. He complained about a terrible stomach ache and rushed home where he remained "ill" for several days. Years later he boasted about his gold-stealing caper, even to Robert Foote, its owner, and displayed a large red scar on his stomach with great pride.

Readers, I acknowledge your righteous indignation over this braggart. However, you must consider the plight of the early-day mine worker. American mine wages ran about $3.50 a day in 1859, the year the gold rush began here in Summit County. In 1904, U.S. mine wages still averaged $3.50 per day although the cost of living had doubled. So some miners felt that fairness demanded they close the wage gap.

Were high graders ever brought to justice? None that I know! If the rascals ever got to court, do you think a jury of their peers, including those grinning Cornish miners, would convict one of their own?

I knew you were a smart reader.

Mine Salters

When a prospector had a worthless claim and greedy dreams of its sale, he faced temptation. "To salt or not to salt, that is the question." Most worthless mine owners responded at once with a hearty, "Yes!" It remained only a question of "how?" A testament to huckster ingenuity are the schemes, ploys, devices, fabrications and sins of omission carried off by swindling prospectors, miners and mine companies in their efforts to pass off passable properties as valuable investments.

Salting is the illicit but widely used practice of exaggerating a mine's prospects by introducing false evidence of riches. Sellers blasted natural gold dust into the barren rock of their lode claims; they filed gold coins down to mix their particles into mediocre placer claims; they poured soluable gold chloride, found in a widely-available 1880s patent medicine, into their mine's unproductive crevices and holes. (The gold chloride in the medicine promised to cure whiskey-caused kidney trouble, a common ailment among boozing miners who kept the remedy on hand.)

Of these three salting methods, blasting gold into rock with a shotgun proved far the best choice because mining engineers often failed to identify the gold as foreign to the mine.

Despite inspectors' flaws, cronies in the mine camp considered any buyer who failed to engage a professional mining engineer to investigate and report on a property for sale a sucker. Among buyers even the smart were duped by gimmickry and their own greed—they wanted to believe claims of riches. But the sucker, the lamb and the rube got eaten alive. Of course, their inspection engineers received royal treatment when they arrived at the mine offered for sale. Right on the heels of the genial "howdies" and lavish compliments came the offer of a bribe.

The shrewd didn't throw money away on bribes. They used their crafty heads. Since knowledgeable mining engineers can identify gold that is not native to a particular mine, placer mine swindlers had to be sure that the color, shape and size of the gold particles they introduced matched those of the claim. When a buyer came to assess the value of an ordinary cleanup at a placer mine, he would probably find a crew of gregarious miners working the sluice box. The inspecting party would insist on personally selecting the spot and the dirt to be "washed" to sidestep fraud.

But a wily crew could salt the selected dirt as they worked. One worker had gold dust in the ashes of his pipe bowl. Another had gold dust beneath his fingernails. A third manned a muddy shovel, its mud impregnated with dust. Sometimes a sweating laborer removed his hat and furtively shook gold flakes from his hatband into the workings. Or he searched for an item in his work pants, shaking out gold into the sluice from a small hole in his pocket. Whatever the trickster's tactic, the end result was restrained joy from a greedy buyer and an offer to buy the claim.

Sneaky tactics didn't always win the day. Silver mines presented challenges to dishonest sellers. Silver ores are complex and difficult to replicate. One ingenious miner, his character flawed by one of the seven deadly sins, avarice, hit on a stratagem. He melted down silver half dollars to salt his mine. He blackened the silver lumps to look like native metal then interspersed them with the mustard-colored syenite rock at the bottom of his shallow silver shaft. Buyer excitement peaked then plummeted when one of the nuggets displayed the printed letters "_ _ _-ted States of."

Hard-rock mine crews like this one at Breckenridge's Brooks-Snider Mine felt justified stealing ore because wages were low.

Sometimes an honest mine owner employed a crew who salted his mine so the workers could continue their employment. And sometimes a swindler's best efforts backfired. A bad egg named Chicken Bill Lovell obtained some rich Leadville ore and scattered it around a barren limestone outcrop back in 1875. Prospectors had just ignited a rush to limestone formations because they had discovered silver and lead embedded in the sedimentary limestone. Chicken Bill scored a legendary "mark" in Leadville magnate H.A.W. Tabor who got sucked into Bill's scheme. After Tabor bought the dubious mine Bill watched in amazed chagrin as Tabor began to take valuable silver and lead from the so-called worthless outcrop.

Salters occasionally got stung and naïve buyers, for whom the mine community could muster no pity, sometimes lucked out. The only consistent factor in the blackleg game of mine sale was the creativity of the crooks.

For example, when mining engineers wised up to shotgun salting, they demanded that sellers blast off the face of the ore-bearing rock. The inspectors could then sample virgin rock. It didn't take long for conniving sellers to pack gold into the business end of the dynamite stick. Thus the new rock was already salted when the unsuspecting engineer studied it.

Inspectors with any knowledge at all identified gold coin filings as salting. And only the tenderfoot engineer believed soluable gold chloride to be genuine. Gold doesn't occur in soluable form. Smart mining engineers got so they knew every trick of the mine salters' underhanded trade.

Any cheater worth his salt, so to speak, would try to outfox that new-found savvy. And the shysters did. They salted the inspectors gunny sacks after they were filled with samples to transport to the assayer. The devious quickly inserted a syringe filled with gold or scattered gold into the sample bag when opportunity presented a chance to open the bag. If all else failed, a garrulous talker engaged the assayer in conversation at the gold ore's final stop, the assay office. When the assayer turned away to find a tool, the imposter quickly salted the ore sample.

Assayers learned to drive off these schemers by opening a container of a vile-smelling compound. The ill-intentioned visitor would run for the door choking and coughing from the chemical dust which the assayer had grown used to breathing.

Assayer tricks like these caused men in the profession of mine salting to seek other employ. Scheming minds can easily shift directions as a Frisco man's story proves.

Oscar Hennick, Dirty Old Man

Brett Harte summed up mine salting and also paved the way for our next shyster, Oscar Hennick, with this verse:

The ways of a man with a maid be strange
Yet simple and tame
To the ways of a man with a mine
When buying and selling the same.

Professor Oscar Hennick began his life of misdemeanor by salting mines then moved on to wooing maidens under false pretenses. In the 1920s, when Frisco had gasped its last in silver mining, Hennick hatched his fraud. A simple and cheap advertisement in a few Eastern newspapers provided all the lure Hennick needed to snare his patsy.

Hennick's early career concentrated on salting Frisco area mines and then through the promising ads enticing Eastern investors to buy these sham ore bodies. The ruse worked for a while, long enough for the Professor to relax his vigilance. Then Hennick's salting enterprise stopped short when a mining expert exposed his schemes. The engineer's name was J.J. Gotch. It should have been J.J. Gotcha.

The newspaper ad, an effective mousetrap, continued to be Hennicks device for a new scam: mail order brides. The so-called professor lured naïve women to travel west to become his bride. Did the smooth-sounding fabricator mention that he was no Romeo but a smelly, vile old cuss?

Oscar Hennick holed up in an old cabin in the Ten Mile. He came to Frisco only when he ran out of grub. Mrs. Lizzie Wildhack, who ran the grocery, suspected the true nature of the old codger's character.

A young lady from Kansas stepped off the train holding the so-called Professor's advertisement for a bride. The pair married but soon the bride appeared back in Frisco, a forlorn tearful figure. Softhearted Mrs. Wildhack gave her train fare to return to Kansas.

Unperturbed, Hennick advertised again. This time the lady, who arrived in town with two grown daughters, stayed overnight at the Frisco Hotel. She had time to pick up the local scuttlebutt on her betrothed's notorious ways. When the unsuspecting Casanova stepped off the Colorado & Southern train in Frisco to fetch his bride, she chased him, pounding his fleeing figure with a club. Her two daughters behind her pummeled the Professor with brooms supplied by the helpful Mrs. Wildhack who knew a mongrel when she saw one. They ran that yelping hound-dog groom out of Frisco.

Speaking of dogs, the hermit Hennick later died in his cabin. Some Frisco men, probably the Demings, went up the Ten Mile canyon to check on him when his cabin light failed to come on at night. Hennick's dog, an aggressive cur, mounted a growling, teeth-baring attack that kept the men at bay. They finally had to shoot Hennick's mean cur to get inside and retrieve the Professor's body.

FIVE: *Drunks, Vagrants, and Bullies*

Traveling journalist Bayard Taylor arrived in 1867 Breckenridge to note the American flag, faded completely white, flying at half mast. Fearing news of national tragedy, he inquired about the half-mast flag. He learned Breckenridge's mournful news: The bully of Buffalo Flats had whomped Breckenridge's best bully, a stout German grocer, a day earlier. In a town devoted to brawls, this defeat brought a noble sorrow.

"Get Yore Hands Off That Gal"

Parkville erupted into bawdy being in 1860 when jubilant prospectors took out $300 to $500 per day from their placer claims there. A bushel of tomatoes then cost a dime. Miners poured into the gulch and the 1860 election rolls recorded 1,800 voters in Parkville. The flourishing mine town soon took its place as social and supply center as well as county seat. The only civilization located west of the Divide, Parkville almost became Territorial Capital in February, 1861, losing the honor by only 11 votes.

All this sudden glory attracted industry and entertainment. Along with the sawmills, general stores and saloons, Parkville had both its own Henry Weiss Brewery and its own mint turning out gold coins. But more than that, Parkville had theater.

Not Shakespeare. No, high hilarity reigned in Parkville and theater was apt to be melodrama at its best and lewd debauchery at its worst. Parkville had three theaters. The Langrishe and Dougherty Theater housed a traveling troupe that toured the mine towns. The actors hailed from Central City and produced many lively shows for overflow crowds. The troupe developed local talent, training miners and dance hall girls to become polished performers. Their entertainment tradition culminated in the Central City Opera House. Later Langrishe and Dougherty's success lured top stars such as Lillian Gish, Frank Fay, singer Eleanor Steber and others to the gold-rich Colorado camps.

Gayosa Hall offered performances by the Colorado Minstrels and more importantly the fetching Mademoiselle Haydee. The Pioneer Theater, housed in a large tent as so many start-up businesses were, offered mine camp revelers their kind of drama.

The reader should remember that these early mine camps had an all-male society. Nightly dances took place but they were stag. Not till later in Parkville's history could the miners shout, "Thar's a gal in the gulch."

Bawdy mine camp audiences sometimes got too involved in the skits. During a melodrama performance at a Parkville theater, a thwarted lover grabbed an innocent heroine and against her will prepared to carry her off. Suddenly a barrel-chested miner, whiskey reeking from his pores, rushed the stage with a loaded revolver shouting, "No you don't mister. Just drop that gal or I'll blow the top of your head off." A panicky change of script soothed the offended miner and the play proceeded.

Zoe Gore

One August night in 1912 a drunken vagrant lurched up toward Curtin Hill (today's Wellington Hill). He planned to visit a house of ill repute. Both Curtin Hill and the red light district on the Blue river's west bank provided services of the ladies of the night. As the drunk stumbled through the intersection, he turned right instead of the correct left.

Just down the street at the Robert Gore home the Daughters of St. John, an Episcopal club for girls and young women, sat primly in the Gore parlor. They stitched as Miss Agnes Finding read aloud from a turn of the century romance novel. Mrs. Mabel Gore sat in the kitchen, absorbed in conversation with a friend. Young Zoe Gore had trouble concentrating on her handwork. She kept an ear alert for sound of her father, Breckenridge's beloved Robert Gore, to return from a long day as dredgemaster of the Reliance gold boat. The dredge had for several days been bucking bedrock, a time-consuming challenge that required him to work late.

A heavy step at the front entry made young Zoe spring up. She hurried to let her father in. When she opened the door, the inebriate, reeking whiskey fumes, got a look at the fresh young miss. His bleary eyes brightened. Lunging at Zoe with breath bad enough to make her dizzy, he roared, "I'll take you, Katie."

The young ladies in the parlor paled in terror when the vagrant chased Zoe through their midst and into the dining room. Hearing the commotion, Mabel Gore, Zoe's mother, rose to her full five foot height and moved into action. She rolled up a copy of her 1900s fashion magazine, the *Delineator,* which was published monthly in a thick size. Mabel charged the dining room, using the magazine as a club and beat back her surprised victim through the parlor to the entryway and out the door, reducing him to pulp on the front stoop.

The Robert Gore home on Breckenridge's Ridge Street displays its front porch where tiny Mabel Gore pummeled a drunken vagrant into insensibility with her rolled up fashion magazine.

Retaining her cool, she set about making hot chocolate for the shaken up Daughters of St. John and served them the soothing drink with cookies to restore their equilibrium.

Robert Gore came on the scene just as his pint-sized wife closed the door on the disabled vagrant. Gore reported the intrusion to Sheriff Jerry Detwiler who arrested and jailed the offender, who turned out to be armed.

Both this story and the next come from a wonderful local book titled *Women As Tall As Our Mountains.*

Disarming Woman

Drunks and vagrants didn't realize what was coming when Mabel Gore stepped into the scene. The tiny matron could summon up the ire of a mother lion when danger threatened. Earlier in 1898 Mabel shepherded her blind mother and two little children onto a railway coach bound for San Francisco. The train rumbled west in uneventful predictability until a loud voice interrupted the calm. A drunk spewing profanities had lurched into the car. As he passed the Gore family, a conductor opened a door, took in the situation and ordered the man to sit down. The drunk would be put off at the next stop. Suddenly the offender pulled out a pistol, and confronted the conductor, leveling his gun at the railway man. Unarmed, the conductor froze.

Mabel Gore, always at the ready when danger struck, jumped onto the red plush seat behind the offender. She jammed her thumb into the man's windpipe with her strong fingers constricting his neck.

"For God's sake, lady, hold tight," yelled the conductor running for help. Mabel held on until a brakeman and other rail men rushed to the scene. The undesirable was off-leaded at the next stop and, Zoe Gore remembered, the train trip continued undisturbed to San Francisco.

Colorow, Bad Boy of the Utes

If Colorow gave the mountain-dwelling Utes a bad reputation, they deserved it for kidnapping him. Colorow wasn't really a Ute after all. Northern Ute warriors had snatched Colorow from his Comanche camp and family when he was a child, ripped him from mother, father and family. That he was ornery for the next 50 years is understandable. That he occasionally turned malevolent, even killing a man in the Gore Range for refusal to feed him, is another matter.

Researchers studying Colorow will be shocked by the bias expressed by writers of his day. They frankly despised him and considered native Americans as savages. They may have tainted Colorow's reputation.

Colorow's noxious reputation may also arise from the gap between good manners by Ute standards versus good manners by American standards, even those of frontier America. For the Utes, to enter a tipi without permission and sit down expecting a meal was to anticipate normal hospitality. When Almeda Peabody arrived in Gold Run Gulch from New York state in 1869 to cook for her brother's crew of miners, Colorow got a huge crush on her. The young woman had long, beautiful blonde hair which the portly Romeo admired. The Ute scared Almeda when he stuck his unwashed head into the cabin window and demanded to Leland Peabody, "I want that squaw." Almeda's brother, Lelon protested, "No good squaw. Lazy squaw."

Did Colorow merely display bad manners? Was he the victim of the raging Indian prejudice of the 1800s? Some view the Ute sub-chief as a leader of a noble Ute people. Others regard him as a treacherous bully. The author stated in her book, *SUMMIT, A Gold Rush History of Summit County, Colorado* that Colorow was a "fat, blustering coward." The town of Dillon apparently agreed when after the book's publication they switched the name of their main street from Chief Colorow to Lake Dillon Drive. Did this tarnish the character of a fine native American? Or was Colorow indeed a rascal?

Let's check in with the old timers for some answers. Consider this tale told by a boardinghouse proprietor, Mrs. Elizabeth Entrekens, recorded in *The Trail* magazine.

Colorow had demanded clothes from Mr. Bailey, a general store owner. The merchant balked at first but finally gave the rotund Indian chief a huge white shirt that Bailey was unable to sell. A delighted Colorow put the shirt on over his clothes and marched over to Mrs. Entrekens' dining room. "Colorow, Injuns, heap hungry," he declared, indicating himself and his small band. The Indians all asked for biscuits which they loved. When plate after plate of steaming biscuits disappeared Colorow demanded "more" and "more." The intimidated Mrs. E. baked furiously. Finally she told Colorow, "All gone." To counter Colorow's protests she took him to the kitchen and pointed to her empty flour bin.

The overweight Indian then waddled to the large communal stew bowl, took the big serving spoon and began to ladle stew into his mouth, "grunting with gusto." An infuriated Mrs. E. forgot her fear of Indian reprisal and cried, "You must not do that, you dirty brute!"

"Squaw no talk. Squaw cook," Colorow replied, continuing to devour the stew.

As the band prepared to depart, Colorow hoisted his heavy person upon his horse and "about a peck" (one-eighth bushel) of still-hot biscuits" cascaded from his oversized white shirt. His comrades gathered the biscuits and Colorow rode away "with stomach well-lined both inside and out."

His enormous appetite for biscuits is a fact remembered by Gladys Shufelt Larsen, an early ranch wife who lived north of today's Silverthorne. She also described biscuits tumbling from Colorow's clothing. It sometimes took two braves who struggled to get the overfed chief onto his sway-backed steed—and then retrieve the biscuits, Gladys said.

Colorow rarely demanded food from men. He waited until the ranchers were away. "He could then threaten the women and force them to cook for himself and his men," Gladys wrote. The ranch wives complied because of their fear of Indians. Colorow only reinforced this terror, according to Gladys. "He had a nasty temper."

A woman who refused to cook for Colorow because she would not toil on the Sabbath reported first "his jaw dropped like a bear trap." Then "his leathery features resembled a composite photograph of the Seven Furies." When a woman stood her ground with the bully chief he often backed down. This time he retorted, "All time Sunday" and slunk away, she said, "hungry, sad and mad."

Gladys Shufelt

Another early-day female who spurned Colorow, Agnes Silverthorn, had little respect for bad behavior. The well-loved wife of Marshall Silverthorn, the judge who presided over the 1860s miners court in Breckenridge, Agnes had almost caused an uprising in Denver. She had approached a squaw who had stolen her bonnet and she shook the Indian woman furiously until the hidden bonnet fell from the squaw's clothing.

In 1862 Breckenridge a large band of warriors had a powwow in town, Agnes Silverthorn's 1883 obituary recalled. (Readers, recall that prejudice flourished in the old days. Insults about other racial groups were commonplace.) The obituary writer declared that the Utes gathered in Breckenridge were manifesting some ugly temper of the savage nature. One of them went to the house and threatened to kill her and her family but the heroic old lady seizing a gun drove away the Indian. The balance of the tribe, appreciating the ludicrous situation of seeing a brave run from a squaw, became good natured without doing any harm.

Another time, Colorow entered Mrs. Silverthorn's Main Street hotel and demanded to eat. She served him at a table by himself away from her boarders. "The ill-tempered savage took umbrage at not being seated with the Americans and grew sullen and insolent refusing to eat whereupon Mrs. Silverthorn shoved him out the back door and as it happened he fell into a hole with about three feet of water." Colorow was "disgusted." But afterward he "manifested much respect for the lady who had so completely vanquished him." And in a rare display he from then on "always paid the regular price for meals when he came in and said 'Heap hungry.'"

The Utes as a people were open-handed and friendly to the prospectors and settlers. They saw treaty after treaty broken and finally endured having their land taken away. They left their well-watered mountain homeland for arid reservations in Southern Colorado and Utah. Colorow and his band marauded Colorado's White River district near Meeker well after the Utes demise here because he escaped the militia escort to the reservation. Settlers had scattered their homesteads. Colorow seized this opportunity to levy tribute from them. He visited the reservation only when annuities were distributed, according to *Denver Field and Farm* in its March 11, 1916 edition.

A huge fiasco began, *Field and Farm* reported, when Colorow's group gambled and lost their goods and horses. To stay in the game,

*Because he was born a Comanche, the facial features of Colorow
(front row, far right) don't resemble those of his Ute Indian band.
Though he scared white women, Mrs. Silverthorn stood up to him.*

they took time out to steal horses from white men nearby. A sheriff's posse summoned to hunt the renegades down exchanged shots with the Utes but no lives were lost. However, the incident revived fears prompted by the recent Meeker Massacre. Stories of atrocities resurfaced. A huge militia formed while furor reigned. Finally at a cost of $100,000, big money back then, and the larger cost of several lives, the routed gamblers were run off.

Events like these may have motivated Hall's 1895 *History of Colorado*, a respected source, to employ unusually flaming language in describing our subject:

> Colorow was a stubborn, ill-tempered, insolent old reprobate. But by those who know his real character he was regarded as harmless and cowardly, a man whom the really brave warriors of his race held in disgust as an unmitigated nuisance.

That Colorow could run from the militia despite his obesity shows some flair on his behalf. At his peak, the Comanche-born Ute weighed 350 pounds. Gladys Shufelt Larson wrote, "Colorow was very fat, very dirty and consequently very smelly, so much so that even his own people objected." Colorow needed a bath.

Perhaps a maiden's scorn, perhaps an amorous interest spurned, who knows why but Colorow took a bath—an open air bath in the dead of winter—and the chubby leader in his tubby made history.

Colorow and his band had watched a homesteader, Jim Conlogue, fill his wooden clothes tub with hot water and proceed to take an outdoor bath. In September. The Indians stared in poker faced contemplation. Three months later in mid-December Conlogue got a summons from Colorow. He rode to the chief's camp to find a naked Colorow dipping his big toe into a pool which the squaws had constructed by arranging a circle of rocks in Turkey Creek. Colorow was demanding they add more hot rocks to warm the icy water. Finally finding it tolerable Colorow submerged his ample person into the steaming tub. Conlogue assumed he witnessed the bath as proof that Colorow could "take it" as well as the white man.

Colorow didn't repeat the bathing ritual before dining with Wolfe Londoner, a well known Leadville and Denver merchant. An early-day wag, Londoner describes the stinky Colorow as a vulgar dinner guest. Londoner, who never failed to savor the humor in human affairs, became a wealthy Denver mercantile leader who lavishly entertained visitors. But in 1860 Leadville, Londoner and his wife had only meager provisions to entertain the voraciously-hungry Colorow.

Readers, to prepare for the Londoner dinner story please digest this bigoted comment from *Denver Field and Farm* on Indian eating habits: "The best fed Indian is always as hungry as a starved coyote. The business of their lives is to dine on everything from a fat dog to a bear steak." Now you can read about Colorow's dinner etiquette:

Londoner had done business with Colorow's squaws, trading their buckskins for sundries they wanted. The merchant invited Colorow to dinner in his California Gulch cabin to stay on his good side. "I was afraid he would take the top of our heads off," he said. Londoner didn't reckon with the ire of his own spouse, a thing to be feared more than Colorow. She pleaded that her larder was bare. When her protest did no good, she created a soup. She must have spiced it with venom. Colorow arrived with several of his squaws and sat down. Londoner recalled:

> I gave the old devil the head of the table. They got the soup but we did not get any soup that day. He would take a spoonful of soup and then spit. He would spit alongside the table. It was the most villainous thing I ever encountered, but durst not say a word.

Colorow later darkened the door of Londoner's store, looking for Wolfe's partner, Dr. Fouts who had gone up the gulch to collect some bills. Colorow addressed Londoner moaning, "Injun heap sick . . . eat too much . . . you give me medsin."

Londoner administered Epsom Salts in a dosage he deemed appropriate for Colorow's size—one tin cup full. The Indian took it and didn't reappear until 7 the next morning looking like a shadow of his former self. "While he had weighed probably 275 pounds the day before," Londoner said, "he now looked like an umbrella cover."

White man heap bad, heap sick, pretty near die, no more medsin," groaned Colorow. When Dr. Fouts returned he was stunned. "A tin cup full of Epsom salts," he gasped, "would kill an elephant."

"Well, it haint killed Colorow," Londoner replied.

Colorow survived to die another day. Hall's *History of Colorado* noted his passing with one ungracious sentence: "Chief Colorow died at his camp at the mouth of the White River near the Uintah Reservation December 11, 1888—regretted by nobody."

Six: *Felony Stupidity*

A colorful character who bungled his way into the limelight, Colonel Lemuel A. Kingsbury, was a head-turning mining man who dazzled onlookers with his 1.5 lb. gold nugget watch chain. Unlike most of the miscreants of history, Kingsbury was never even a petty criminal. A well-known and normally-savvy mining man, he gains inclusion among this book's miscreants for one brilliant misjudgment. His error falls into the category of felony stupidity.

Lemuel Kingsbury and the Water Grab

Kingsbury's first plan was to debut a luxurious pleasure resort above the Iowa Hill Placer, also called the Banner Placer, on today's Peaks Trail near Breckenridge. In the author's hiking guidebook, *The New Summit Hiker,* she described it this way:

> The man-made lake here, part of an idyllic turn-of-the-century summer resort developed by Colonel Lemuel "Nuggets" Kingsbury, was stocked with trout in 1904 in preparation for the debut of his Iowa Hill Resort on "Banner Lake."

When the resort failed to make a go, Kingsbury turned in 1905 to a grand mining project called Buffalo Placers, located in Salt Lick Gulch just south of today's Wildernest subdivision. He built the wooden flume visible from the I 70 interchange on Frisco's Chief Mountain.

This costly and extensive flume would divert water from the North Ten Mile—and you can still see Kingsbury's old wooden pipe along the hiking trail there—to wash gold from his gigantic placer operation.

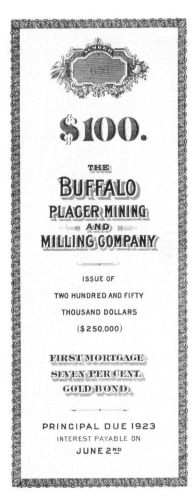

After much expense and publicity, the Colonel stood ready to turn on the water. Waiting ranchers from "down the Blue" then arose as one to say, "You can mess with our wives, but that water is ours and you better not touch it."

Oops. No water rights, no water available and no placer mining, which depends on plenty of water.

Colonel Kingsbury was undismayed by this embarrassing oversight. He was a staunch turn of the century American capitalist with all the idealistic vision and Don Quixote style faith in commerce that characterized the era. He wore a derby hat and a three-piece suit and under it a genuine pot belly, not what old timers called a stuffed shirt. That was padding to make a gent look wealthy enough to be able to overeat.) Kingsbury's gold watch chain lay across that pot belly, commanding enough to earn him the nickname "Nuggets."

Dillon-based Buffalo Placers Company mined into the 1930s.

Interviewed in Denver on his way to Boston to meet officials of his mine company, the magnate tossed off a few comments about his memorable watch chain. "Yes," he said, "I guess this chain is about the only one in the world of its kind. It's worth nearly $400 at mint prices and at nugget prices more than twice that amount has been offered for it but I wouldn't sell it for any amount."

Some of the nuggets on the chain stood out. One presented "the exact profile of Senator Cannon of Utah." At the chain's end lay an unusual sylvanite nugget the Colonel called alternatively "Bryan" (a controversial politician) and "Judas" (betrayer of Christ) because, he said sarcastically, both were fond of silver. Sylvanite combines both gold and silver in a single specimen, a stunning item.

Breckenridge locals knew where these showy nuggets came from—the Blue River's Mecca Placer.

An expert in placer mining—the retrieval of free gold by washing it from creek gravels—Kingsbury managed the Mecca. He sank a 27-foot shaft there to access Blue river bedrock His effort aimed to reach an old channel of the river. When Kingsbury's men reached the old channel, they ran a "drift" for about 40 feet and hit a bed of gravel. It proved to be what the November 29, 1900 *Denver Times* called "a show for the entire district." The gold came out in spoonfuls, handfuls and cupfuls. The gold chunks, once washed, were shipped to New York City and displayed in a Broadway store.

Some of these notable nuggets glittered in the Colonel's watch chain.

That same news article reveals Kingsbury's theatrical bent. He could hornswoggle the unsuspecting. A favorite trick of his was to stroll into a hotel lobby and lightly set down his two suitcases at the front desk. When the bellman tried to lift these bags after Kingsbury registered, his eyes, and maybe a hernia, bulged. The *Times* explained,

Rich placer mines owned by expert miner Lemuel "Nuggets" Kingsbury yielded specimens for his legendary gold watch chain.

"In his valise he carries about $5,000 worth of nuggets and ore 'for small change.'"

Clearly the *Times* reporter was dazzled. He began his report by glowing, "The Mecca has made a record which excels anything heretofore made, even in Breckenridge, which is no stranger to phenomenal outputs from placer mines."

At the present $400-plus per ounce in 2005, the gold's worth would be $20 million—impressive baggage.

All this publicity drew Kingsbury attention but he eventually earned the wrong kind of attention. A series of hate letters to his eastern backers in 1908 labeled the mining man a "hypocritical fraud." The *Summit County Journal* deplored the accusation.

> Colonel L. Kingsbury for a number of years has been bringing in considerable eastern capital to open up and equip placer mines in this county . . . In promoting as well as actual mining he has been fairly successful. But he is now harassed and hampered by some enemy in Denver who is writing blackmailing letters to the eastern associates. These letters, adroitly written and widely circulated, pretend to warn all prospective investors against separating themselves from their money.

At the time of the damaging letters Kingsbury had neared the end of his career. Born in Georgia January 22, 1847, he was then 61. Kingsbury and his wife endured the bad publicity and remained in Summit County. He continued to manage the Buffalo Placers Company from his Dillon headquarters. The company worked as late as 1934.

Kingsbury's well known daughter, Marian, was a musician with the Metropolitan Opera in New York City. She left the opera company in 1914 due to World War I and opened a music studio in nearby Leadville. She remained there through the time of Kingsbury's death April 26, 1921 from pancreatic cancer. Colonel Lemuel "Nuggets" Kingsbury lies in the Grand Army of the Republic section of Breckenridge's Valley Brook Cemetery.

A larger than life character full of a sense of capitalist idealism, Kingsbury had big dreams and many of them he achieved. He earns inclusion in this book only for an amusing lapse.

Rev. Florida F. Passmore, Brash Crusader

Striding into the community, Methodist Reverend Florida F. Passmore preached repentance to the town's sporting element. Passmore resembled another repentance messenger, the New Testament's John the Baptist who had his head chopped off by a drunken King Herod. Passmore inspired similar retaliation. Revenge came from both Breckenridge revelers and Methodist church authorities.

What sin did the new Fr. Dyer Church preacher commit? He campaigned for and won enforcement of Colorado Saloon Law closures in Breckenridge. Irate miners united to rally against him. Passmore also condemned his superior, Colorado's Methodist bishop, for lavish living. And while he still had a head of steam he accused the Bishop of consorting with "the lowest slum element." For this audacity the prelate put Passmore on church trial.

The Colorado Saloon Law, enacted April 7, 1891, required that saloons close at midnight on weekdays and all day Sunday. Both saloon keepers and imbibers considered the law nonsense and failed to obey it. To cut off Breckenridge's raucous gaiety as early as midnight was considered unthinkable. And the miners, who honored Sunday by refraining from work, reckoned as outrage restrictions that kept them from enjoying their Sabbath rest in the congenial atmosphere of the saloon.

The only person who regarded the Saloon Law as a blessing direct from heaven was the fire-breathing reformer, Rev. Passmore. He visited each of Breckenridge's seven saloons to warn them of impending doom. Then he demanded that Sheriff F.F. Brown enforce the new law.

That action earned Passmore the rank of public enemy number one. The *Summit County Journal* on August 1, 1891 labeled the law ridiculous: "The law was conceived in the brain of a fanatic, enacted by a body of imbeciles, signed by a doughface and in a camp like Breckenridge would be enforced only by an impractical enthusiast."

Journal editor Jonathan Cooper Fincher called Passmore "unChristlike" and lambasted him as a "non-taxpaying, Sunday-working temporary resident" who behaved like a bull in the town china shop. The *Dillon Enterprise* joked that barkeeps who ignored closure times should be sentenced to three Sundays of hearing brother Passmore preach the gospel.

Undaunted, Passmore pursued his cause. He insisted that law officers who failed to enforce the Saloon Law must forfeit their bond, effectively putting the Sheriff and his deputies out of a job. In a letter to the editor championed by Breckenridge's party crowd, Sheriff Brown scalded Passmore: "You avoid the facts as satan does holy water."

Passmore responded by pressing charges against popular saloon proprietor Johnny Dewers for violating closure law. After hearing speeches by defense witnesses, Passmore "finally shook the American flag until the eagle screamed," according to a blatantly biased news article. An equally biased jury decided in favor of Dewers.

Their revenge unquenched by the court decision, the miners carried out their own justice. On August 17, 1891 they employed their savvy with dynamite to remedy the problem. They blew Passmore's proud new church bell to bits. And like the blasting professionals they were they demolished the new belfry as well.

By October the unshrinking Rev. Passmore had ordered a new bell, this one 200 pounds heavier than the first.

In the end Passmore achieved his unpopular goal. In August 1891 Breckenridge saloons shut their swinging doors at midnight on weekdays and all day Sunday. Miners who came out of the hills and gulches spent their Sundays mournfully lounging on the town streets.

Success went straight to the saintly head of the Methodist church pastor. He next dredged up an 1866 Gambling Law and insisted Breckenridge's cherished faro, keno and poker games be abolished. Both gentlemen and common laborers held their gaming privileges as sacred.

They hung Passmore in effigy. The preacher received an ominous letter advising him to get out of town, or else. Passmore stood his ground.

An athletic man who taught boxing in Breckenridge—except on Sundays—Passmore had the edge over many a potential assailant. At six feet, six inches and 250 pounds, he loomed like an Old Testament Goliath over the trembling Israelites. "An ordinary man might as well tackle a bear," early day observer Ed Auge stated. Plus that, he had the power of his convictions. He backed up those convictions with his fists.

Despite the malevolence of the Breckenridge miners, the pastor enjoyed the support of his Methodist flock during these well-publicized incidents. Attendance at church and participation in church programs flourished during the saloon closure debacle.

And debacle it was. By March 1892, standards relaxed. Breckenridge saloons again stayed open till the wee hours and supplied the traditional solace to miners all day Sunday. Gambling also resumed. A sense of order returned to Victorian Breckenridge.

Rev. Passmore, energized by his Breckenridge battle, went on

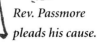

Rev. Passmore pleads his cause.

to bigger challenges. This time he turned his sights toward leaders of his own Methodist Church. He accused the Denver-based bishop of the Colorado Methodist Conference of complicity with the liquor traffic. His reasoning: Methodist clergy preached prohibition but voted the Republican ticket. The Republicans, along with the Democrats, favored licensing saloons which sent Passmore's blood pressure skyrocketing.

These charges "convulsed" the clergy's summer meeting, according to the June 12, 1895 *Rocky Mountain News.* Passmore gave the clergy "a severe drubbing," the *News* said, then turned his attention to Colorado Governor John Evans. Passmore scored the governor for "running street cars to make money on Sunday." He failed to consider, one assumes, that the faithful might need public transportation to get themselves to Sunday worship.

The Methodists censured Passmore for what they called "lies" but he declined to be silenced. "The fiery reformer replied," according to the *News,* "that he refused to stop speaking the truth."

The brash reformer had tweaked the devil's nose.

To shut him up, Bishop Warren scheduled an 1896 church trial for Passmore in Leadville. Passmore grabbed what he saw as divine opportunity. With the spotlight on him and a center stage position provided by the Almighty, Passmore rose to the occasion. Before reporters and an audience of influential church hierarchy, he railed against Bishop Warren for being in league with saloon-keepers and drunkards, neatly summarizing that the Bishop was more guilty than the sinners themselves.

Along with the church spotlight, Passmore seized another divine appointment. Interest in his case in Leadville ran high, so Passmore used the notoriety to preach to great crowds in the Leadville streets. Heaven supplied the opportunity.

Meanwhile, inside the courtroom divine favor failed to prevail. Passmore was convicted of "immorality," (defamation of Bishop Warren) and expelled from Methodist ministry. Tranquility returned to Methodist religious life.

Passmore retreated to Rifle, Colorado where he became a circuit preacher. Far from the publicity melee of Breckenridge and Leadville, he enjoyed acceptance and success. But his fervor arose again to insure his defeat. In 1896 he attempted to seize a Grand Valley church and its congregation from Methodist control. Following this Passmore had to be physically thrown out of a quarterly Colorado Methodist Conference meeting, probably no small job considering the misguided reverend's strength.

Passmore turned up in Denver in 1898 ready to create a fuss. He mounted a soapbox against the Methodist church, declaring that a man cannot be a Christian and still belong the to Methodist church, which is "unworthy, corrupt and sensual." The intrepid muckraker then turned on Bishop Warren again, denouncing his then-costly $35,000 mansion. In fairness, he also assailed prominent Denver pastor, Dr. Coburn, for a fancy $200,000 Grace Methodist Church building. Passmore advanced his brash attack. He accused rich church donors, for whom the front pews were saved, of consorting with back pew shop girls, whom the church should protect. In a July 3, 1898 *Denver Times* article, Passmore issued a threat:

> Dr. Coburn a few nights ago told how some working girls lived on $1 per week and in his front pews sat men who impose on these girls who have to clothe, feed and heat themselves all on $1 per week. And I must not say a word about it. Certainly not while these men worship in the $200,000 church . . . If Bishop Warren and Dr. Coburn strike these poor people, I will strike them with all my might.

Methodist chronicler Isaac Beardsley later wrote in *Echoes from Peak and Plain,* "In all that he has done, he claims to have Divine approval." Like John the Baptist, he confronted the Victorian double standard of preaching holiness and tolerating sin. He suffered persecution for justice's sake, just as the Gospel Beatitudes suggest, and never backed down from his righteous cause.

Rev. Florida F. Passmore stayed in Colorado. The 1920 federal census places him in Denver at age 76. Born in Georgia August 12, 1844 and raised in Tennessee from age six, Passmore had come to Colorado in 1879. The 35 year old lived in a tent in Alma and took up mining. Rev. J.R. Shannon discovered him there, impressed by his unpolished but passionate sermons. Licensed to preach in 1880, Passmore served flocks in Alma and Fairplay. The Methodist church ordained him in 1888 at age 45. They kicked him out of ministry eight years later.

Looking back on his life, one concludes that his offense was one the firebrand reformer failed to see in himself: The sin of presumption.

Seven: *Womanizers, Debauchers, and Seducers*

B reckenridge town mayor and Breckenridge town masher. Business leader and
lecher. VIP and viper. Who better qual-
ifies as a pillar of society that Charles Augustus Finding? Rich merchant, prominent mine owner, father of virtuous daughters who
formed the Sisters Mustard Seed charity—that was Charles Finding.

Charles Finding, Philanderer

To understand his character, and lack of same, let's look at
Charles Finding's life. A promising young Britisher who proved himself in the banking business in Denver, Charles yearned to have his
own mercantile business. He launched his first store in1872 Fairplay.
From there he moved over Hoosier Pass to Breckenridge after managing to marry that town's most sought after maiden, Martha Silverthorn. Daughter of the popular hotelkeeper and judge of the miners
court, Martha Silverthorn came from a respected family.

In Breckenridge Charles Finding first partnered with a man
named Dimick to sell groceries and general goods, then launched

Finding Hardware as sole proprietor. The hardware store became a prosperous business offering mining supplies and equipment just as the boom in hardrock mining detonated. He leveraged the store's profits to invest in local mine properties. Later Finding expanded to Denver's hotel and hardware business and owned the Railroad Block, one of Denver's first fine office buildings. He became both a recognized leader in Breckenridge town affairs and a well-known Denver businessman.

Finding's wife, a black-eyed beauty and tough-as-hardware-nails Colorado pioneer, raised the family's three daughters in a Victorian home on Breckenridge's Main Street.

Tall, muscular and handsome with his chiseled features, the social pillar Finding was, alas, a notorious womanizer. A philanderer. A libertine. A wolf. The local newspaper, reported on his seductions of another man's wife and flirtation with a floozy. In typically florid early 1900s verbiage, the *Summit County Journal* scalded our hero with a burning editorial quill: "He degraded himself . . . became a menace to common decency . . . a stench in the nostrils of society . . . a social vulture who parades in human form."

Yet Frank Hall in his esteemed *History of Colorado* calls Charles Finding "solid and successful . . . a good citizen." Wilbur Fiske Stone's 1918 *History of Colorado* praises Finding's "keen sagacity, sound judgment and determination."

Which is true?

Young Charles Finding

Let's delve deeper into Finding's story so you can decide yourself.

Charles Finding, born February 22, 1850 in St. Ives, England, came to America at age seven with his parents Joseph and Eleanor (Tomlinson) Finding. The family settled in Newark, New York. After school at 17 Charles entered the Bank of Monroe in Rochester. Tuberculosis brought him to dry Colorado in 1870. Recovered, he took his first job as a bookkeeper for the then well-known early Coloradoan Wolfe Londoner. Later he took charge of accounting for a young Colorado National Bank, his 1927 obituary later recorded.

Finding had the incredible luck to meet and woo Miss Martha Ralston Silverthorn, whom he married on January 16, 1873 according to the *Rocky Mountain News*. The young couple took up residence that same year in Fairplay, the May 9, 1873 *News* reported. Finding opened his general store on Front Street.

"C.A. Finding, postmaster and dealer in everything has about doubled the former capacity of his building and now has it full of groceries, provisions, hardware, clothing and 'everything else,'" said the *News*.

Charles and Martha moved the mercantile business to Breckenridge probably in 1874. Finding possessed a gift for making money. Later the *Summit County Journal* reported, "he made a fortune here." An expensive wedding gift to Martha's sister, Matilda Silverthorn at the time of her April 9, 1879 marriage to the prominent General Joseph Wilson, demonstrated that money-making talent. The Findings presented the couple with a pearl card case and a solid silver thimble.

By January 18, 1880 the *Denver Daily News* mentioned that Finding Hardware had enjoyed marked sales in a month formerly characterized by dismal sales. Breckenridge, mostly inhabited only during the summer months, experienced its first year-round season in 1880 when the lode mining boom began.

"Mssrs. Dimmick (sic) and Finding, one of the business firms, state that they are selling more goods now each week than at any time during the summer in a month," the *Daily* said.

Spring 1880 saw the number of buildings in a formerly sleepy Breckenridge jump to 300, "tents included," according to a May 2, 1880 newspaper report on mushrooming growth. "The grocery firm of Finding and Dimick heads the list in that line. A stock worth $25,000 has been sold for cash, since the excitement commenced. These gentlemen have several mining claims on Nigger Hill, the *Daily* added. Nigger Hill is now called Barney Ford Hill after the Breckenridge black pioneer.

Finding often traveled to Denver, even before the railroad arrived in August, 1882, an era when primitive stagecoach travel taxed the endurance of many passengers. The May 4, 1881 *Rocky Mountain News* lists Finding as a guest at the Grand Central Hotel. On March,12, 1885 he stayed at the St. James hotel, among other visits. We assume his Denver visits were *strictly* for business.

Breckenridge, a town of 500 according to the 1880 *Colorado Business Directory*, had seen its population triple by 1882 to 1,500. Finding and Dimick, selling groceries and hardware, benefited from this 1879-launched boom for five good years.

Then on a cold December evening in 1884, tragedy struck. A defective flue in Finding Hardware's chimney caused a conflagration around 5 p.m. that jumped from structure to structure. Denver newspaper reported placed the loss estimate at a stunning $75,000, big money in the 1880s. The fire burned the Grand Central Hotel, wiped out the businesses of H.H. Irwin, W.H. Woodside, Ed Radigan and Mr. Newcomb, plus about 15 smaller buildings. With Firemen's Hall almost next door, hand-drawn fire equipment manned by Breckenridge's three fire companies controlled the huge blaze by 10 p.m. The *Summit County Journal* on December 11, 1884 reduced the loss estimate to $50,000, still significant in the 1880s when a lunch cost five cents. Shocked by the devastation of his building and inventory of goods, Finding vowed to rebuild in stone. The new Finding Hardware, a building still standing at 120 South Main Street, was made of local rock and native sandstone.

Perhaps the prosperous 1880s mining output compensated Finding for his loss. He owned a number of mines including the Hammer Lode, northeast of Farnham on Boreas Pass; the Governor King near Lincoln in French Gulch; and the notable Briar Rose on Peak 10. "Six men are taking out two cars of ore a day for Finding and Company" at the Hammer Lode, the *Denver Daily News* announced on March 12, 1885. Finding's Governor King had "a rich vein of ore from thirteen inches to six feet."

Financial success could never compensate Charles and Martha Finding for the death of their little daughter, Ada, who succumbed to diphtheria of the larynx in 1888 at age 12. Before her death Ada started Sisters Mustard Seeds, a charitable and educational girls' group that lasted 35 years.

Twice elected mayor of Breckenridge in 1882 and 1888, Finding participated in civic and social events. The 1890s saw the bicycle become all the rage. Finding and his daughter Agnes joined a party for a full-moon bicycle excursion to Dillon and back. Afterward "the group danced at Pore's hall for several hours."

Always athletic, Finding traveled over Boreas Pass during the Big Snow Winter of 1898-99 with his daughter Tonnie. (This trip included a 1,500 foot altitude gain through very deep snow!) Snow buried buildings above their rooftops and no supplies came in by rail for 79 days that winter. But a news clip reports a supply trip by sled: "R.B. Stapp and C.A. Finding and a party of ladies and gents are using sleds to go to Como 24 miles."

Mr. And Mrs. Charles A. Finding, an upcoming young couple, prospered from the 1880-launched lode mine boom. Despite Charles' dalliances, they later marked a 50th wedding anniversary.

By the early 1900s Charles Finding used his mining investment earnings to buy a half interest in Denver's Albany hotel in addition to his hardware business there. He also owned the railroad-tramway building at 15th and Larimer Streets. Martha later sold the property to the tramway company for their construction of a loop there. This property may have been the Silverthorn land acquired when the family lived in Denver in 1860.

Life began to unravel for Charles Finding in the 1890s. He snared a $1,200 contract from the Summit County Commissioners to build a jail. He met a tight deadline, beginning construction on October 17, 1899 with a deadline of November 10, just three weeks. Despite the jail's up-to-the minute steel cells encased in granite, the jail leaked prisoners like a sieve. According to Susan Donaldson in *Summit's Courthouse,* prisoners escaped with sickening regularity until the new courthouse with its basement jail opened in 1909.

Finding's jail couldn't hold lawbreakers and Finding's social stature could no longer stave off the truth about his character. The first *Summit County Journal* story on Finding's dalliances blared this headline:

LAWYER'S HAPPY HOME BROKEN UP

The story detailed Charles Finding's year-long adultery with a married Southern lady.

It began in January 1905 when a Kentucky couple, H.C. Clay and his attractive wife Lillian, arrived in Breckenridge. Mr. Clay joined the local Elks Lodge, one of several popular Breckenridge fraternal organizations. There he met the rich and prominent C.A. Finding. Clay introduced his new Elks "brother" to his wife. Charles Finding, enamored by the charms of this Southern belle, not only lost his heart but also his Victorian inhibitions. Despite his mature age of 55, his 30-year marriage to a fine woman and his role of father to his daughters, Finding beguiled his way into the Southern lady's boudoir on a regular basis. The affair lasted from October, 1905 to November, 1906. That's when Mr. Clay returned unexpectedly from a six-week business trip to Kentucky and discovered Finding in a most compromising position with his wife Lillian.

The story was all Breckenridge could talk about. Clay confronted his wife and she confessed every detail, according the November 17, 1906 *Summit County Journal*. She "told me exactly how it was, when it was, how it occurred and all about it," a distressed Mr. Clay told a courtroom audience. "She openly confessed to adultery with one Charles A. Finding, a merchant of this town."

Although the custom of settling gentlemanly disputes with a duel to the death had passed from common practice in these parts, the South still held to this hallowed tradition. "I sent word to Mr. Finding to put on his gun." Clay strode up Breckenridge's Main Street to Finding Hardware and paced back and forth awaiting the duel. No Charles Finding. When he could no longer contain himself, Clay entered the hardware store where a clerk placated the agitated attorney with news that Mr. Finding had gone to the bank and would be right back. Clay waited.

Charles Finding, who in fact had not gone to the bank, failed to show up to engage the rules of Victorian gentlemanly justice. Instead of appearing at the front door of his hardware store to meet his challenger, he bolted through the back door. With rascal's luck, he found the Colorado & Southern narrow gauge rumbling along the track and jumped on the caboose.

The old-timers had a name for people like Finding: *Lily-livered knave.*

The newspapers jumped on this juicy story, calling it "a luscious story of duplicity and dishonor." Meanwhile, a strained and grief-torn husband and father pleaded his cause to a hastily-assembled divorce court. H.C. Clay told the court that he wished to avoid "reflecting upon her . . . but I have two children and some property. I feel that I should protect my children by obtaining at this time a divorce." In the case of his untimely death, the children, not Lillian, would then inherit his property. Clay summed up by saying, "I am heart-broken."

The three-man jury, Charles R. Auge, Mario Cook and Loren Chapman, promptly decided on divorce. Clay sold his house and personal property, closed his law office, collected his two children and departed for London, Kentucky leaving Breckenridge and its most prominent citizen in his dust. He carried with him, the November 17, 1906 *Journal* said, "the sympathy of 98 percent of the town."

Lillian Clay boarded the Colorado & Southern to return to her family home.

If you readers think this is the end of the story, it's not. Just you wait.

A few months later, H.C. Clay came back to Breckenridge. When his shock wore off, lawyer Clay sued Charles Finding for $25,000 in damages for alienation of affection. Clay won but the amount was negotiated down to $1,725, a figure agreed upon by both parties. However, Charles Finding neglected to pay. Clay brought another suit in 1907 to collect the $1,725 and this time Finding demanded a change of venue to Denver, claiming that Summit County would never give him a fair trail. In a move guaranteed to earn him more ruinous publicity, Finding accused the *Journal* and the *Breckenridge Bulletin* in 1907 of "poisoning the minds" of potential local jurors.

Denied a change of venue, Finding, whose resources for legal action came from a deep pocket, gave the newspaper editors the surprise of the decade. The large type of a September 7, 1907 headline trumpeted,

SUMMIT COUNTY PUBLISHERS ARRESTED

Last Sunday afternoon two deputy sheriffs from Denver arrived in town with criminal warrants, from the district court of Denver for the arrest of O.K. Gaymon and J.W. Swisher, publishers of the two Summit county papers.

The literary prisoners, detained as they were enjoying the Sabbath, were summarily dragged off to the Leadville jail. (As the reader will remember, the Charles Finding-built Breckenridge jail had a swiss-cheese type construction flaw.) The warrants charged the publishers with criminal libel. Though no complainant's name appeared on the warrants, the publishers "infer that one C.A. Finding is the party aggrieved."

Goading the press drew a tirade of abuse. Editor Gaymon wrote,

Charles A. Finding, the English bully, is fast finding out that some of the courts of Colorado are ready to step in and thwart his devilish desire to have the publishers of his home papers thrown in jail for daring to tell the truth about him.

On last Tuesday Judge Cavender, the able lawyer and fearless jurist from the bench, told Mr. Finding if he had any grievances . . . to bring action in Summit county, where the offense, if any, was committed.

But fairness and justice is not what Mr. Finding is searching for. It is to humiliate and financially ruin the afore-said publishers . . . He, according to his own statements, has money to burn and is willing to separate himself from a wad in order to jail us.

While toxic verbiage flowed, do you think that a remorseful and chastened Charles A. Finding mended his philandering ways? The answer is a resounding, NO!

Just eight months after Finding was found with Mrs. Clay, he made sordid headlines in Denver and Breckenridge newspapers. During a Flag Day outing in Denver's City Park, a Breckenridge lady with her husband and children was enjoying a dish of ice cream under the pavilion when her little girl became sick. Trying the door of the ladies' toilet, they found it locked. After a long wait, the little girl grew worse. The mother pounded on the door. Finally she summoned a policeman who demanded the door be opened at once.

The door opened and out stumbled Charles Finding grasping a half-filled bottle of whiskey. A blonde woman with a partially filled glass of booze in her hand oozed out the door behind him.

Finding escaped to Breckenridge to avoid the Denver publicity only to have another event of pounding on his door. This time it was Sheriff Detwiler, serving him with papers on the Clay alienation of affection lawsuit.

A Breckenridge newspaper responded to the story saying, "It is all old history to Breckenridge—the record of this degenerate and libertine. We have his record with other women and his Denver record is a peach."

Regarding Finding's libel suit against them, the publishers retorted, "His character can't be libeled."

The situation culminated with an encounter outside a Breckenridge blacksmith shop when another prominent businessman, outraged with Finding's business practices, planted a right uppercut square into Finding's mouth, knocking him down as though he'd been kicked by a mule.

Finding, his chiseled features rearranged, boarded a train bound for Denver with his false front teeth in his hand and a visit to his dentist uppermost in his mind.

His assailant pleaded guilty to assault and battery, according to the newspaper. He was fined $3, "this being the minimum penalty."

Despite his reputation as a cad and bounder, Finding managed to stay married to Martha Silverthorn Finding. In fact a July 17, 1923 Denver newspaper displayed the couple's formal portraits under the headline, "Pioneers Fiftieth Wedding Anniversary."

In Charles Finding's defense, we need to record that his daughter Charline Antoinette "Tonnie" died at age 28 on October 24, 1905, the same month that Finding began his affair with Lillian Clay. Losing a second daughter must have caused him terrible grief. However many people lost loved ones during that era of epidemics and killer diseases like pneumonia, but did not behave like Charles Finding in response. But certainly Tonnie's death made him more vulnerable to temptation.

Charles Augustus Finding died alone in his room in a Denver hotel in 1927. (Martha, his wife, passed away in March, 1931.) His obituary, and probably his eulogy as well, described his life in illustrious terms. Historian Wilbur Stone, writing in 1918 after his amorous shenanigans, called Finding a "wealthy, influential and respected man."

Edward D. Traylor, Lecher

This story allows no room to poke fun. It involves a premeditated crime. Edward Traylor, the wealthy manager of the Royal Tiger Mines Company in 1919 forced intimacy with a 16 year old girl from a well-loved local family. She concealed the resultant pregnancy from her down-the-Blue ranching family until late February, 1920 when her baby son arrived, shocking the girl's mother into an unconscious state.

Ed Traylor's brother, John A. Traylor had organized the Royal Tiger Mines company in May, 1917. Traylor had purchased the rich

IXL Mine in the Swan Valley to start the mining enterprise. The company town of Tiger quickly arose. Company benefits made Tiger the Summit County place to live and work. Electricity, a steam heating plant and a water works meant easy street to workers used to braving cold both inside and outside their log cabins and frame homes. Tiger, located five miles east of Highway 9 on the Tiger Road, provided a good school, a boardinghouse, a bunkhouse, office building, assay office, a large ore mill and blacksmith ship, plus Oliver Swanson's sawmill. Dr. W.G. Smith offered medical care to the 250 Tiger residents.

Free motion pictures and dances spiced up leisure hours. Rent, light, water and medical service were all free.

One of the employees enjoying all this early 1900s easy street convenience was Chris Cluskey who also owned a ranch north of Dillon along the Blue River. Cluskey had emigrated from County Meath, Ireland in 1900. He worked as head team master with 18-horse teams to oversee. Ore hauling gave way to transporting the bodies of influenza victims during the global 1918-19 flu epidemic. The affable Chris wangled a Tiger job for his then 15 year old daughter. Mary Ellen Cluskey waitressed at the Tiger commissary during mealtimes and sorted ore the rest of the day. Mary, full of life, loved to pick wild berries, enjoyed her friends and adored dressing up for dances in Dillon and at Slate Creek Hall. "Name any kind of dance and we did it," she recalled later.

Her job at Tiger provided needed income but almost immediately brought trouble. She caught the deadly flu virus not once but three times and managed to survive in a time when obituaries took over the front page of local newspapers. She also caught the eye of the 60-ish Ed Traylor. He managed to get his wife to hire Mary to work in her boardinghouse. Mary began fending off Traylor's seduction attempts. The grandfatherly Traylor, as the employer who signed both

Mary Ellen Cluskey (back row far right in jacket) joins workers at the Royal Tiger Mine Company in the Swan River company town.

Mary's and her father's paychecks, held a powerful position in the young girl's life.

On June 6, 1919 Ed Traylor allegedly drove Mary in his motor car to her family ranch down the Blue. The rape occurred that day.

Incredibly Mary was able to conceal her pregnancy from her family. Fashion had abandoned the corset and tight waist for loose-fitting dresses. In February, 1920 when pains beset the young girl, a bewildered family summoned a doctor to help. The doctor announced that the Cluskey daughter was in labor. According to a later news account, Mrs. Lizzie Cluskey fainted at this report and did not come to until after her grandson was born.

Mary confessed the assault to her parents and named Edward Traylor as the father and perpetrator.

Perhaps because he had noticed Mary's pregnancy (or perhaps not) Traylor, a longtime Breckenridge resident, suddenly left town in

November, 1919 before the child's birth, citing business concerns in Allentown, Pennsylvania.

On Friday, February 20, 1920 the Cluskey family brought charges of statutory rape against Edward Traylor. A *Denver Post* headline announced:

Rich Mining Magnate Held On Charge by Girl Who Becomes Mother at 16

The *Summit County Journal* refrained from publishing the story till the *Post* revealed the facts. Then the *Journal* report, included in the local history *Blasted Beloved Breckenridge,* said:

> With great reluctance, we publish the fact that Breckenridge has a sensation—a scandal—the gravity of which, as the facts come out, threatens to place an old man, gray with age, past the age of 60, before the public as a licentious debaucher of the chastity of females of tender years, and to stifle the life of one of our brightest and most promising high-school girls.

Summit County Commissioners held a hurried meeting to see if county finances could bear the cost of an extradition. Deciding yes, they dispatched Sheriff Detwiler to Denver to await extradition papers. Governor Shoup was to preside over an extradition hearing but that hearing failed to take place. The Summit County district attorney, Eugene E. Bond traveled to Denver, a thick file of pro-Cluskey witness affidavits under his arm. He failed to budge the governor. Power players needed time work behind the scenes. Delay after delay occurred. The local D.A. traveled a second time to Denver. Finally the *Summit County Journal* broke a page one story on March 6, 1920 announcing that Edward Traylor had been arrested in Pennsylvania. The *Journal* noted Traylor's position in the community: "Traylor has been a resident of the Breckenridge district for years and in addition to his business connections has been prominent both politically and socially."

The defendant hired a phalanx of high profile attorneys, including former Colorado state attorney general Leslie Hubbard; former Summit County district attorney Barney L. Whatley; Ralph Hartzell; and William R. Eaton. They charged that their client was the victim of a blackmail frame-up by the Cluskey family.

The attorneys obtained a change of venue for Traylor. The rape case was tried in Leadville. At the trial the final day of February, 1921, a spate of contradictory witness statements befuddled the jury. After an all-night session the jury emerged from deliberations to declare themselves unable to agree on a verdict. The curious throng which packed the Leadville courtroom went home frustrated. So did the Cluskey family.

However, a later re-trial proved conclusive. The powerful Edward D. Traylor ended up in a prison cell at the Canon City penitentiary with a sentence of 10 to 12 years.

Traylor died in the penitentiary nine years later.

Mary Ellen Cluskey married Bill Ruth in 1926 and led a happy, busy life. The couple worked as caretakers for the Tutt family of Broadmoor Hotel fame at their enclave on beautiful Uneva Lake in the Ten Mile Canyon. Mary served as Frisco postmaster. Tragedy loomed when her son Bernard was reported missing in action in World War II. Her brother Chris had been killed in the conflict. Happily, Bernard was released from a Nazi prison camp and returned to his mother at war's end.

Cpl. Bernard Cluskey, Mary's son, wrote from the war, "Mom, I've been through Hell."

Mrs. Cluskey never fully recovered from her blackout over the shock of Mary's sudden labor and childbirth. She spent many years as an invalid but a cheerful invalid whom neighbors and friends called a "saint" because of her giving nature and happy attitude.

Dr Joseph F. Condon, Lily-Livered Knave

Small town gossip probably inflamed the hatred between Breckenridge's prominent Dr. Joseph F. Condon and its well-loved local barkeep, John B. Dewers. Dr. Condon maintained a flourishing practice as a local physician and invested in high-profile mines. Johnny Dewers, a German immigrant and longtime resident, enjoyed the camaraderie of presiding over his Corner Saloon on the northwest corner of Lincoln and Main.

The dispute between these two men arose from Dr. Condon's reputed affair with John Dewers' wife. Rumors of a liaison between Condon and Mrs. Dewers had long dominated the Breckenridge scandal mill. When Dewers looked out his saloon window to witness Dr. Condon handing a note to Mrs. Dewers in the street, Dewers thought the worst. Indeed the alleged infidelity led to the Dewers' divorce, a singular event in the Victorian 1890s.

Even more unusual, the romance ended up in the news columns of the *Summit County Journal.* On August 6, 1898 editor Oren K. Gaymon wrote:

> For some time the social and moral sentiment of the community has been tinted with scandal, but whether or not there was a grain of truth in the rumors is yet to be proven, but the reproach figures as factors in the separation and divorce of Mr. and Mrs. Dewers.

Patrons of Breckenridge's Corner Saloon at Main and Lincoln favored Johnny Dewer's home brewed Cherry Bounce and enjoyed his genial hospitality.

Mrs. Dewers left Breckenridge for Stockton, California after the divorce but animosity between the two men continued to seethe. On August 4, 1898 while summer wildflowers painted the hillsides and rare warm weather prevailed, the dam of rancor burst.

A chance encounter between the adversaries sealed the fate of both. Dr. Condon was treating a patient who needed a tooth pulled and the physician came into the street from his Main Street and Lincoln Avenue office seeking the dentist, Dr. Elgin. Spying Condon from his window, Johnny Dewers rushed from the Corner Saloon and demanded that Condon "square the old score."

J.F. Condon took John Dewers at his word. The doctor drew his 38 revolver and pumped four shots into the unarmed Dewers. "In rapid succession, he fired," the *Journal* reported August 6, 1898, "causing almost instant death." With anatomical precision the doctor aimed the first ball into Dewers' neck, the second into his right side and the third to his heart. A fourth "went astray."

As Dewers lay dead in the street, Dr. Condon calmly walked up Lincoln Avenue, turned onto Ridge Street and proceeded to the county jail where he surrendered to Sheriff Jerry Detwiler.

The *Journal* bemoaned the tragedy:

> The shooting was one of the most unfortunate occurrences that could have happened in the town. Both were prominent citizens and bore excellent reputations. The doctor is from Michigan, married, and, with his wife and sister, resided happily in their pleasant home on Washington avenue, and had built up a lucrative practice in his profession.
>
> Perhaps there was not a more popular man in the county than Mr. Dewers; big hearted, free, congenial, enterprising and a general leader and favorite among the young men of the town, who loved him as they did a brother. He was an active and honored member of the fire department and a prominent Red Man.

John Bernhard Dewers died at 37.

Life had taken a tragic downturn at the onset of the 1890s for the popular saloonkeeper. Dewers and his wife lost their 17 day old baby Anna on June 25, 1890. Less than a year later, a second infant died at 16 days on June 8, 1891. Later came Mrs. Dewers' affair with Dr. Condon, then Dewers' untimely death at the doctor's hand.

Breckenridge reeled. Tranquil for a decade, the town had seen no homicide since Reddy Stuart had killed Pat McCarty in 1888. Two of its finest citizens had now succumbed, one to a heinous act of crime, the other to tragic injustice and death.

Dr. Condon enjoyed the privilege of membership in Brecken-ridge's clubby Warm Stove Mine, a tight bunch of town business and professional leaders who gathered in George B. Watson's men's fur-nishings store to swap tales of mining feats and hunting conquest. These men postured in their three-piece suits and important hats, invested in mining ventures, influenced local politics and basked in social acceptability.

Getting to the Warm Stove Mine was easy for Dr. Condon who kept his medical office above Watson's store on the southwest corner of Main and Lincoln, directly across from Dewers' Corner Saloon. Condon, a large, homely man with protruding ears, displayed a hint of melancholy in his countenance—hardly a dashing swain. He lived in the fashionable Victorian home at 111 East Washington first built for black pioneer Barney Ford in 1882.

Saloon proprietor Dewers had come to Breckenridge as a teenager. When a June 11, 1880 forest fire nearly destroyed the town he worked with others to establish a fire department. The group built Fireman's Hall and Dewers joined the Pioneer Hook and Ladder Company as a volunteer firefighter. Johnny Dewers became a naturalized American citizen on July 31, 1884. He served as fire chief in 1892 and '93, before The fire laddies mourned his death, calling him "our beloved and esteemed brother" in a published Resolution of Condolence.

Johnny Dewers' funeral, held on Saturday after the Thursday shooting, drew a crowd too big for the large Grand Army of the Republic Hall to accommodate. The weekly *Journal* on August 13, 1898 summarized:

> The funeral of the late John B. Dewers held on last Saturday afternoon was the occasion for the populace to show their appreciation of their once beloved citizen. The auditorium

being filled to overflowing, hundreds of citizens could not gain admission. The several fire companies were out in uniform and with the (Order of) Red Men marched to the cemetery where the last rites were conducted by the latter order.

With Dewers buried in Breckenridge's Valley Brook Cemetery and Condon installed in the more secure Leadville jail, District Attorney Sam Jones brought formal charges against the doctor in Judge DeBarneure's court. The complaint charged the doctor with "the willful and premeditated murder of John B. Dewers." Dr. Condon hired Denver lawyer E. A. Richardson, along with C.A. Wilkin and Judge Clark of Breckenridge to defend him. D.A. Sam Jones asked for and got a high bond amount: $10,000.

The judge set Condon's trial for October in district court. It is interesting to note that a Mr. R. DeBarneuere happened to be the defendant's partner in their shared Pacific mine investment. A group of prominent Breckenridge men donated the whopping $10,000 cash to get Dr. Condon out of jail.

Townspeople inflamed by fierce loyalties to one or the other of the enemies were about to face a second startling crime: On Thursday, August 11, 1898, just one week after Dewers murder, the felon Pug Ryan and his gang robbed the gentlemen enjoying the gaming room of Robert W. Foote's Denver Hotel. The gang relieved the gents of their diamonds, ornate gold watches and other jewelry treasures. In a later effort to arrest these robbers, a violent gun battle took the lives of two well-loved local men, Ernest Conrad and Sumner Whitney. (See page 138 for Pug Ryan's story.)

Summit County, a small community, was stunned by the loss. Next to the *Journal* news column detailing Condon's crime ran a story reporting the bold robbery.

One more blow awaited the distressed community. Ready to unleash a history-making blast of storm and nonstop blizzards was the Big Snow Winter of 1898-99. Dr. Condon's trial, scheduled for October, was continued to November 1898, the month that launched the record-breaking snows. Most activity, including the railway's delivery of food, mail and news, came to a snow-clogged halt that winter. Dr. Condon's trial didn't take place until the snow began to melt in mid-May, 1899.

Condon's attorneys, the prestigious Richardson and Clark, successfully argued that a fair trial for the physician could not be had in Breckenridge. A change of venue to Fairplay in Park County was granted. Fairplay received its initial naming by 1860s miners as Fairplay, expressing hopes for a town without foul-play, claim-jumping and other injustice. (Readers, please remember this fact for later.) About 50 Summit County residents attended the trial. The *Journal* called the populace "much worked up over the outcome."

How Sheriff Jerry Detwiler made the trip over a wind-beaten, blizzard-pounded Hoosier Pass to Fairplay on January 12, 1899 for Condon's hearing is a challenge to the imagination. The lawman's cryptic entry in the Sheriff's Docket Book indicates that he traveled 44 miles that day at a cost to the county of $17.90, a large sum by docket book standards. The delay of the trail till May rendered his harrowing trip unproductive. A bill for an even larger sum, $655.55, arrived from Park County after the trial as one of the expenses of the Condon-Dewers affair.

Well over a century later, stories of the murder still circulate. And questions remain. Why would Dr. Condon, who had already wronged Dewers in an alleged affair with his wife, also murder the man he had offended? The reverse, Dewers pumping bullets into Condon, makes a more realistic picture. An argument for self defense, despite Dewers

Gunshot victim Johnny Dewers rests in Breckenridge's Valley Brook Cemetery beside the graves of two baby daughters.

being unarmed, prevailed during the four-day Condon trial in Fairplay.

Joseph Condon had a chance to tell his side of the story at the trial. He insisted that the note he handed to Mrs. Dewers in April, 1897 actually came from a Mr. Miller who requested that he pass it to the lady. Condon testified that Dewers had given him cause to fear for his life. He recounted an incident at the Thanksgiving dance where Dewers bumped him several times and tried to pick a fight. Condon asked the marshal to accompany him home that night.

Condon also stated that he "received warnings from McGarvey, Riley, Watson, Foote and others that Dewers was going to do him up," the May 15, 1899 *Fairplay Flume* reported. The *Flume* recorded Condon's statement about the events of August 4, 1898, the day Dewers died:

> On the fatal 4th of August, 1898, he had attempted to pull a tooth for a patient, but failed, and started to find the dentist himself and was going up the street when Dewers came out of a building, grabbed him, and went to pounding him, saying "you son-of-a-b-, I'll settle with you now."
>
> Condon attempted to ward him off with his hands and told him to keep off. As he backed off the sidewalk he received a kick from Dewers in the stomach, which made him very sick, he tried to vomit, became bewildered and stunned and continued to retreat to the center of the street. Dewers advancing and

Dr. Joseph Condon (seated at left in light-color hat) is no dashing Romeo.
Did he murder his lover's husband, the popular Johnny Dewers?

pounding and kicking him all the time. He became possessed
of great fear, and when Dewers' hand dropped by his side he
thought he was going after his gun and would kill him.

"I got out my gun as quickly as I could and fired as fast as
I could, and I found afterwards by examining the gun that I
had fired four shots."

A jury of his peers, bleary-eyed from late-night deliberation,
issued this verdict for Dr. Condon at 9 a.m. on May 19, 1899:
Not Guilty.

But Breckenridge remained divided. Kind, congenial Robert
Foote, who first collected cash for Condon's $10,000 bail and was
subpoenaed as a witness for his defense, pledged to never speak to the

doctor again. Moreover, the death records in the St. John's Episcopal Church where John Dewers attended services expressed the people's verdict. The detailed notation of Dewers' death by murderous gunshot is smudged out. Obviously the church disagreed over the jury decision. Finally St. John's leadership replaced their earlier two line description with the bold letters of one word:

    KILLED.

Mrs. Condon takes a stroll on a footbridge near Breckenridge. Her calm life in the Barney Ford house changed when Condon faced court trial.

Author's Note: Dr. Condon and his wife, Laura Argue Condon, enjoyed a pleasant and prosperous life in Breckenridge following the acquittal. Mrs. Condon's 1900 Valentine party for the glee club drew a distinguished crowd. The doctor continued his practice, receiving appointment as county physician in 1902. He changed his newspaper ad, which earlier showed his office location as "one door north of J.B. Dewers," to "over Watson's store." In 1905–06 Dr. Condon saw "great success" in the Morning Star Mine which he worked with William P. Condon and Dr. E.W. Shrock. Dr. Condon died on December 5, 1915, 17 years after shooting Johnny Dewers.

EIGHT: *Four Flushers and Imposters*

The author tells J.H. Myers' story through the persona of Frank E. Wire, an annoyed business rival who endured a barrage of criticism from the Colonel.

He came here to Frisco uninvited in the late '90s and stirred up a hornet's nest of lies. I'm just one honest mining man stung by the Colonel's high falutin' fibbery but I'm not the only one. Don't quote me but I was glad when Frank Cherryholmes popped that silver-tongued slicker in the nose. And yes, I admit I helped Frank pay his fine from the Frisco town board after the hearing.

Colonel James Havens Myers, Double Dealer

Let me back up and introduce myself. I'm Frank E. Wire, president of the Square Deal Mine. Our silver property is located up the North Tenmile crick just past the beaver ponds on Chief Mountain. Our honest mining practices have suffered a continual barrage of false and slanderous accusations from this same Colonel Myers. Instead of making his own mines produce, he busies himself damning every law-abiding mineral enterprise that competes with his King

The Square Deal Mine drew the slur "Crooked Deal" from its detractor,
Colonel J.H. Myers—to the exasperation of mine president Frank E. Wire.

Solomon Mining Syndicate, a gimmick organization he made up
back in 1878 to promote his own gain.

I can in good conscience claim that every charge of fleecing
investors and every allegation about our issuing false bills of lading
that he trumps up against us is part of a clever smokescreen to divert
public attention from his own double dealing.

Wouldn't any man with real red blood running in his veins feel a
twinge of jealousy? Here's the situation: Myers elbows his way into
Frisco, uninvited I might add. He got burned out in Chihuahua—the
town destroyed in that murderous fire of '89—so he's looking for new

pastures, you might say. He proceeds to throw ill-gotten money around and buy up every known mining property in the Ten Mile Canyon almost overnight. He buys himself the say over town matters with that same bankroll.

Wouldn't it wear on a man when train car after train car of rich Eastern investors rolls in to take the Colonel's four flushing mine tours? Those greenhorns get taken in themselves to boot! Wouldn't it rankle a genuine professor if someone waving around their own published book on mining comes in advocating a newfangled idea about "deep mining" and the whole world listens to him—not to the established miners of their own district?

And how can a man compete against a slick promoter with a built-in soapbox? The Colonel has eased himself right into the job of newspaper editor in Montezuma and uses the *Prospector's* columns to hurl printed accusations at his competitors with dishonest abandon. Even before he got himself control of the newspaper he was sending out a volley of letters and news items to editors in Frisco and Breckenridge.

I returned his fire with some well-aimed letters of my own to the *Breckenridge Bulletin.* Those letters contained the true facts about the Square Deal Mine. I countered in particular the slur he broadcast calling us the Crooked Deal Mine. But nobody can get the last word in with a high-flown fabricator who wields the editor's quill in his shameless double-dealing hand.

Even when he's not the editor, Myers has his way with those newspaper writers. Listen to this hypocrisy:

> Colonel Jas. H. Myers, mining promoter par excellence, visited this newspaper's offices Monday last with news about gold strikes in his Chrysolite Mine near Chihuahua. Gold is rare in this silver district. Colonel Myers, perched on this editor's

Three shifts of workers labored round the clock to drive the King Solomon tunnel for deep mining proponent Colonel James H. Myers. It exceeds a mile in length.

desk, dripped quotable mining quotes as easily as his cigar dripped ash. A golden tongue have the angels given this harbinger of prosperity in "the Halls of Montezuma."

Glorified rubbish! But I'm trying to have my say as well. Ed Huter—he's my superintendent at the Square Deal—Ed added some particulars about Myers' shady deals in Cleveland to my last letter to the *Bulletin*. The editor there put a flaming headline on it: "Frank E. Wire Goes After Myers' Scalp." Myers fired back in print "Show me one bill of lading for an ore shipment." That vein in my neck bulged when he had the audacity to accuse me of exactly the tactics he uses himself. Look at this humdinger: "Frank Wire promotes and sells fraudulent stock to investors."

Well, my response showed up once and for all his promoter greed and exposed him as a knave. He answered back like some lofty philosopher with this memorable quote, "The promoter is the John the Baptist of industrial development." I say, humbug!

Myers himself plays the holy Catholic on Sunday mornings then the rest of the week schemes up devious ways to break the ten commandments, including *Thou shalt not steal.*

Let me show you the stack of newspapers and fraudulent mining brochures I've collected on Myers. Why, I've got my proof right here. Look at this fancy printed mining prospectus book that J.H. Myers himself put up for his King Solomon Mining Syndicate. See this: There's the Jessie mine and mill, richest property in the famously rich Gold Run Gulch near Breckenridge. See, he doctors the pictures to place the Jessie right across the road from his Mint Mine, which is in fact a useless hole in the ground right here just south of Frisco. That's an outright lie!

This is the same holier-than-thou Colonel who publishes his "Ten Commandments for Businessmen" under his monicker *de plume*, "Old Quartz." He preaches about smelling out phony mine brochures, as if his own aren't a mess of pottage:

A pole cat is know by its smell; a porcupine by its quills; a jackass by its bray and a wild-cat mining company can be spotted by its literature.

Now if that ain't enough for you, roll your eyes across this front page to the *Summit County Journal*. Right here a town board member from Frisco exposes the four flushing manipulation and downright falsehood Myers practiced. He should have spent his time producing silver ore for his investors.

*Though pictured in mining clothes, the persuasive Colonel could
don a three-piece suit and smooth-talk investors into staking their
mining investment cash in his King Solomon Mining Syndicate.*

See here where Myers and his brother-in-law, Elijah K. Bailey, tricked Frisco town trustees into believing their claim that the pair acted as agents for the railroad. They then acquired in their names some Frisco town lots earlier dedicated to the railroad for right of way and buildings during railway construction days. Look here it says, "Bailey came out here from Iowa three or four years since and, with no other credentials than his and Myers' word, claimed to be the officially appointed agent of the railroad to divide and receive a deed to its share of the forfeited lots." And it says, "Bailey secured a deed as trustee for the railroad to these lots." Why, that's cheating as plain as the nose on your face.

Myers, of course, sermonizes from his newspaper pulpit:

You may reform the thief, the drunkard or the libertine, but the liar is beyond redemption.

He goes as far as to quote from the Bible itself, that old prophet Jeremiah. Myers is warning no other rat than himself with his high-minded verses. This is the favorite of that old hypocrite:

A sword is upon the liars and they shall be dismayed. Jer. 50:36

Look here where the town trustees tell that when Myers first came to Frisco he got himself elected a town official—clerk and recorder. They say the truth will out. Get this: His first job was to research into those forfeited lots he later hornswaggled for himself. Then see where it says the town came up short on the cash Myers managed as clerk. The Colonel insisted that the loss resulted from "irregularities" which irregularities the trustees claimed came from "Myers' own manipulations during his incumbency as clerk of the town."

Here's the letter from the Frisco official. Says right here, "In his letter Mr. Myers, as is his wont, poses as an injured innocent. But Myers' complaint in the incident proves him the vulnerable party. The rock must have hit Myers, for he's the only one squealing."

Have you seen anything as sanctimonious as the Colonel's response? He takes the chair of the high professor, talking down to his detractors here:

The man that lacks energy to excite a protest—the devil does not want him and in Heaven there is no room for him. The great achievements of this world have been accomplished against the protest of the multitude.

Myers claims, drones are to be pitied more than dead men," drones being persons who don't have his conniving mind to steal those Eastern lamb investors blind. Myers has the undiluted gall to point out that Civil War leaders like General Ulysses S. Grant himself incited controversy and the fate of great men is to draw brickbats. He's trying to cover up his devious doings by saying that great men draw criticism. He's being roasted, not for being a great man, but for being a four flusher.

Now I know you're thinking, Colonel Myers by himself revived Frisco mining when he launched his syndicate here in 1898. And his theory of deep mining has since been proven by experts. And he fought that environmentalist Gifford Pinchot who wanted to limit mining in national wilderness parts. Insanity, that was. And he drove that Vidler Tunnel to be the first in diverting water from the Colorado Western Slope to the Front Range. Yes, he did accomplish all that. Nevertheless, I'll be glad if that big strike north at Green Mountain takes him away from Frisco.

Myers was said never to turn down a friend—or to forgive an enemy. Maybe that last part is a trait of the Colonel's that I'll use on him.

—Frank E. Wire

Frank E. Wire
PRESIDENT.

Author's note: Colonel Myers' achievement as the pioneer who first peddled water from these mountain rivers to the Front Range contains an irony. Myers initiated the first water diversion from Summit County. But water diversion forced him out of his final Summit County resting place. He died in 1923 and was laid to rest in the Old Dillon Cemetery. Dam construction forced his relatives to disturb those restful bones in 1962 when Dillon Reservoir swallowed up the Blue River and spit it into pipes going to Denver. The new lake displaced the Old Dillon cemetery, and the old Colonel with it, so they trucked his remains to Buena Vista's Mount Olivet Cemetary.

Stephen Decatur, Inscrutable Imposter

The author has written this using the persona of Grace Greenwood, a well-known woman writer of the 1880s and an intimate of Stephen Decatur.

Imposter, yes. Bigamist, indeed. Liar, I grant you that. Eccentric—wildly so. Stephen Decatur was a rapscallion to be sure. But he was also a fascinating personality, fresh and full of surprises—a man I'll never forget.

I am Grace Greenwood. You may recognize my name as an authoress. I was also the confidante of Stephen Decatur, an irresistible and perplexing character. I admit that I am not the only woman Stephen wooed. But I believe he loved me best.

For years loyalty demanded that I keep secret things that Stephen whispered only to me. Now that he has died, I will tell his story. I would stay silent but Mr. Frank A Root, in his history, *Overland Stage to California,* has pulled the cloak of mystery from Stephen's true identity. I now add my part, only because others need to recognize the richness of his character.

He was a flawed genius to be sure. My mother told me I didn't know how to chose a man. She may have been right. Stephen Decatur

Stephen Decatur first trudged over the Divide to Peru Creek in the 1860s.

posed as a man he was not. He married and deserted several wives and families. He refused to acknowledge not only his brothers but his own sons and daughters. And he lived his life in a bizarre freedom, to the bewilderment and grief of many who loved this charming enigma.

I first met Stephen when I was 22. He had slogged through spring snow over the Divide from Georgetown into Summit County's Peru Creek valley. He wasn't sure where he had ended up. "Is this Greenwood's Hole on Peru Creek?" he asked, stepping into the dark, windowless tent saloon, blinded from the bright outdoors.

"Who's askin'?" my pa retorted. "Er, the name's Smith," Stephen replied. "John Smith." "Nope, it ain't," Pa corrected. "We already have more'n a dozen John Smiths on this crick." "Ah, yes, I see," Stephen said, twinkling his eyes merrily at me. "That would be confusing."

"Pull y'self up to the bar, mister," my pa said, "and pour y'self a drink on the house." At the same time he shoved a big syrup can toward the stranger. "Here's the alias can. Pick y'self out a diff'rent name. None of us got no patent on that monicker, John Smith, but further indulgence in it will lead to monotony and puzzlement. We picked a bunch o' names out of a history book and mixed up the front names and the hind names, then wrote 'em down on pieces of paper, trimmed off the *Rocky Mountain News*, and put 'em in this 'ere can. That way mentalities that can't come up with nothin' more original than John Smith for an alias can git themselves a high soundin' name."

With a grin of amusement, Stephen plucked a scrap of paper from the syrup can. "Ulysses S. Washington," he read. He paused. Pa brought out his persuasive powers, saying, "Most of these men are dead now but they're still good names cuz they made it into the chapter on American battles. As veterans, they deserve somebody bein' named after 'em. We mixed up the front an' hind names cuz this is a law-abidin' settlement and we won't have no infringement of the copyright law with that history book we used."

"Wal dagnabit," Stephen declared, mimicking Pa right to his face. "That's a helluva good name but I guess my real one is a sight better. Shake hands with Stephen Decatur."

"Let's likker," cried Pa, spilling more whiskey into Stephen's cup. "I like to meet an honest man. Now I advise you if'n you want to prospect this gulch, and prevent an untimely passin', to keep on bein' honest. The boys here don't want no sheriff nosin' around here. Fact is, nearly everyone camped up here has a past they don't want the law lookin' into. So we aim to keep the gulch moral. Murder, claim jumpin' and larceny in any form, along with skullduggery, is punished by hangin' after a conviction by a miners meetin'. All other offenses is winked at."

Stephen flashed me a smile that melted my insides. "What's skull-duggery?" he asked laughing. "Skullduggery is any criminal infraction that ain't included under the category of murder, claim jumpin' or larceny," Pa responded.

"Well, I'm as moral as any Quaker," replied Stephen with a broad wink in my direction. "I won't be bringing the law to Peru Creek. I'm here to claim a townsite and put up a real town here so reputable business folk such as yourself can count on steady patronage."

"Two drinks call for a third," declared my Pa. The two talked the whole afternoon long and Stephen entertained us with stories of his Mexican-American war adventures, with keen observations about people, his enthusi-

An aging Stephen Decatur, the "prince of prospectors and character of characters," disowned his family.

asm about new western land and his dream to build a roadway over nearby Argentine Pass. He spun tales of traveling with the Mormons, who I later learned tolerated his plural marriage practices but broke with him over his drinking. He related anecdotes from his youth, about his birth in Sussex county, New Jersey and learning the trade of shoemaker from his father, Joseph Bross. The family once lived near Milford, Pennsylvania and Stephen received an education at Williams

College. I got a glimpse into his personality as he quoted from old Greek philosophers, famous Americans, poets and books of the Bible. I told myself that I would get an education myself and some day hold my own with the engaging Stephen Decatur.

And that's just what I did. I studied at the Academy in Denver and later became a writer. But no story character I created every matched the versatility of Stephen Decatur. A famous author, Samuel Bowles, came to Colorado in 1868 and wrote a book he called *Colorado, Its Parks and Mountains.* In it he called Stephen "the prince of prospectors and the character of characters"—an apt description.

My prince charming, too charming for his own good, also demonstrated a need for adventure so strong that he abandoned his wife and family to seek it. When Stephen left his first wife, Evalinda, she was expecting their second child. I make no excuses for him. He lied to her saying his job as headmaster of Chester Academy there in New York state required him to travel to New York City. When he failed to return and no trace of his whereabouts turned up, Evalinda with Stephen's brothers and family mourned him as a victim of murder in some dark city alleyway.

Instead Stephen had deserted his predictable Eastern life to follow Horace Greeley's call, "Go West, Young Man!" When a son was born to Evalinda, the tearful widow named him Stephen Decatur Bross to honor his departed father.

But Stephen had dropped his family name, Bross, even before he arrived in Colorado in 1859, the first year of the gold rush. A few years later the burden of his secret, and too much whiskey I imagine, caused him to confide in Mr. Frank A. Root. Mr. Root served as an express messenger and agent for the post office department. He wrote Stephen's story in his *Overland Stage to California.* I have kept Mr. Root's book with me. His says the following about Stephen:

In the spring of 1864 I met at Latham station a queer genius and talked several hours with him. The name that this gentleman went by was "Commodore" Stephen Decatur. I did not talk long with him until I learned, from his remarks, that he was born in Sussex county, New Jersey. Being an Eastern man myself—a New Yorker by birth—he was free to talk with me and seemed glad of the opportunity. I soon observed that he was man of remarkable conversational powers and that he was possessed of a fund of valuable information. I also learned from his own lips that his elder brother was Lieutenant-Governor Bross, of Illinois, whom many will remember as at one time the managing editor of the Chicago Tribune.

The "commodore" lived for many years in his native state, where he taught school, but one day in the 40's he told his wife he had to go to New York, and he left his home, and was not heard from again. Subsequently he drifted out West but dropped the name of Bross. While on the frontier he enlisted in General Doniphan's regiment, and seemed proud of the fact that he was one of the men who made the famous march under Kearney to Santa Fe and Chihuahua. Later he settled on the banks of the mighty Missouri and for several years ran a ferry between Council Bluffs and Omaha. He was approached one day by his brother, who recognized him, but he denied his identity absolutely.

In 1859 with a throng of study pioneers who, because of the gold discoveries on the eastern slope of the Rockies, made their way from the Missouri river to the mountains, he went to Colorado, where he lived and where he finally died.

From the time he went there his manner of life was well known to all the pioneer citizens of the Centennial state. During

the Civil War he early enlisted as a member of the Third Colorado Regiment and participated under the gallant Colonel
Chivington, in the memorable fight at Sand Creek, in which
engagement some 600 Indians were slain and the death of 174
whites between the Missouri river and the Rocky Mountains
was avenged.

As a soldier the commodore was as brave as he was gallant.
He was a conversationalist whom it was a pleasure to meet. He
was widely and favorably known as a citizen, a forcible
speaker, and a man of education, with most of the refined
instincts of a gentleman. For a time he was editor of the
Georgetown Miner and for a number of years the prospected
about Georgetown in Clear Creek county and about Peru and
Montezuma in Summit county, and in 1866-'68, represented
that prosperous mining district in the Colorado territorial legislature. At the Philadelphia Centennial Exposition, he ably
represented his adopted state. During this time it is said he was
recognized several times by his relatives, but always denied his
identity. Delegations of citizens from his old home, it is
alleged, called on him and established his identity by marks on
his person, but he maintained his stolid denial.

When one of his brothers, William Bross, who later became Illinois Governor, learned that his long-lost brother Stephen was alive
and well in Colorado, he made the trip west and searched out
Stephen's home on a ranch. The *Chicago News* verified what Stephen
himself confided to me.

After a perilous journey across the mountains he reached
Decatur's ranch. Judge of his astonishment when he was met

at the door by a buxom Indian squaw, who told him that she was Mrs. Decatur. Mr. Decatur was not at home, but the governor, now sorely perplexed, resolved to await his arrival. It was not long before a sturdy mountaineer came striding up the road. One glance informed Gov. Bross that it as indeed his brother and he ran out with open arms to greet him.

"Stephen, my brother," sobbed the governor.

Stephen recalled to me that his brother fell upon his neck, weeping with joy to see Stephen restored to the family. Stephen (and this amazes me as it will you) disentangled himself, stepped back and growled, "Sir, I do not know you."

Governor Bross was dumbfounded but asked Stephen if he did not have a scar on his left arm a few inches above his wrist. In response to this question, Stephen coolly rolled up his sleeve to display the scar. Despite this confounding behavior, Stephen treated his brother with his warmest hospitality and marked kindness. After many pleadings for Stephen to unbosom himself, and finding his entreaties continually repulsed, Governor Bross departed a disappointed man.

In typical Stephen Decatur unpredictability, he later took a strong fancy to his brother's daughter who also visited. Shortly after refusing her father, Stephen took her on a camping trip down the Blue River and delighted in showing her the picturesque scenery of his mountain homeland.

Stephen had added the title "Commodore" to his name as a joke when he ran a Missouri river ferry from Omaha to Council Bluffs. He took the name from a renown hero of the day. The true Commodore Stephen Decatur, distinguished at Tripoli and a popular military idol of his day, later lost his life in a duel with James Barron. Stephen picked up his title to add pomp to his assumed name and amusement to his life. The title puzzled his family but everyone in Colorado called him "the Commodore."

I laughed with him about the title and I forgave him for the squaw and his several other wives, a string of outrageous bigamies. Stephen was a passionate man who needed women in his life. The *Georgetown Miner* acknowledged this in an 1888 article after his death, saying: "He was a Byron among the women, ever ready to make love to any and all." I liked this comparison to the passionate British poet, Lord Byron. I am less pleased to disclose that in 1856 after he distinguished himself in Doniphan's regiment and the march to Santa Fe and Chihuahua in the Mexican War, and received praise from the head of his company, Colonel Clay Taylor, he returned to illegally marry a woman in Decatur, Nebraska, a town he founded. Stephen gained recognition there as a speaker, outstanding citizen leader, good shoemaker (his shoemaker father had trained him) and man of education He fathered three children. Then he abandoned his family to travel west to Colorado where he arrived at the onset on the gold rush in 1859.

Before his unannounced departure, however, Stephen spoke at a public meeting near Omaha in 1857 or '58. David H. Moffat, one of his Chester Academy students, recognized Stephen and informed a second brother, John A. Bross, a prominent Chicago lawyer. He at once started for Nebraska. Stephen met his brother with a deadpan look and an indignant refusal to acknowledge him. John A. Bross later died on a Civil War battlefield.

Stephen's soul was stirred by the gusto of the gold rush. Adventure, a new start, challenging primitive conditions and seams of gold and silver in colossal mountain ranges gave Stephen the test he always needed. He immersed himself in mountain life with his characteristic enthusiasm.

As soon as 1867, his leadership earned recognition by his election as Summit County clerk and recorder as well as his August, 1867 election as Summit County's representative to the Colorado Territorial Legislature. In 1869 he built Argentine Pass, which scaled the Continental Divide at more than 13,000 feet, from Georgetown to Summit County's Peru Creek valley and the town of Decatur that he established there. The road construction proved harrowing with much loss of life among the workers due to the steep precipices alongside the route.

Stephen became associate editor of the *Georgetown Miner* in 1869 and composed lively articles for that newspaper for four years. History credits Stephen with the 1870 naming of the town of Silver Plume, just above Georgetown. He took pen to hand to honor the new camp with this poem. (Of course, he doesn't fail to mention the ladies):

> *The knights today are miners bold,*
> *Who toil in deep mines' gloom!*
> *To honor men who dig for gold*
> *For ladies who their arms enfold,*
> *We'll name the camp Silver Plume.*

In 1876 Stephen received the high honor of the Governor's selection as representative from Colorado, the new Centennial State, to the United States Centennial Exposition in Philadelphia.

This is the Stephen Decatur I hold in my heart. We remained friends—and more than friends—from the day I met him in my father's tent saloon on Peru Creek. I moved in and out of Stephen's life until his craving for alcohol dominated his personality. At first his secret drinking amused me. He gave a speech in Georgetown at McCoy Hall on temperance which brought his audience to its feet. Afterward, the *Miner* intoned, "If everyone should follow the precepts of our speaker, there will be no drunkenness in our land." How we laughed together over our whiskey about that remark! His favorite toast summed up the dichotomy of his character, "Here's to our noble selves. There are few like us—and few like us."

I believe that alcohol provided Stephen an escape from guilt over his early misadventures. He knew that his first wife, Evalinda, had learned he was alive. Now in 1888 an aged lady, she faithfully raised his children and always remained only his wife. His daughter married Benjamin Nelson, a prominent merchant in Binghampton, New York. His son, Stephen Decatur Bross, grew into a fine man.

Of Stephen's three children born in Decatur, Nebraska, one son, Godfrey, survived. Born in 1863, he is now 25 and lives in California with his mother, a fine Christian woman. Shortly after Stephen left her, a second brother visited and convinced her of Stephen's bigamy. I understand that the news caused a sorrow from which she never recovered. Stephen had other children, several of whom he met and delighted in but he refused to acknowledge them as his own. Several of his children live in Chicago today.

Remorse over this tragic neglect led, I believe, to Stephen's alcoholic demise. He died alone and nearly destitute in obscure Rosita, Colorado in 1888.

A *Georgetown Courier* obituary on June 7, 1888 a few days after his death mentioned my name. "We know of but one person to whom he may have confided the story of his life. If he did, our readers may some day see it from the pen of Grace Greenwood."

Today is that "some day."

I will never forget.

—Grace Greenwood

NINE: *Thugs and Felons*

A week after the popular Johnny Dewers' funeral (see page 108 for his shooting) a notorious thug blasted bullets into two of Summit County's cherished citizens. The murders followed a jewelry heist at Breckenridge's elite Denver Hotel. No one ranks higher on the roster of wrongdoers than the infamous Pug Ryan who masterminded the crime. Ryan stands as a robber, murderer and blackguard.

Pug Ryan, Ruffian

Some of Breckenridge's staunchest citizens played a role in the Pug Ryan affair. They were his victims, divested of their watches and jewelry while engaging in a little innocent gambling the night of August 11, 1898. The hold-up itself proved mild by the standards of the old West, but a violent gun-battle followed. The bloody deaths of two local men, both husbands and fathers, and two outlaws, forever stamped Pug Ryan's name on the memory of Summit residents.

Breckenridge's well-bred Denver Hotel enjoyed typical Saturday night business. Faro, roulette, crap and stud poker games amused patrons of the hotel's game room. Bartender Ed Brewer scurried about in white apron, serving foaming schooners of beer and other spirituous beverages. Chips clinked, cigar smoke wafted toward the ceiling, conversation buzzed, the bar bell rang.

Suddenly a band of four miscreants, masked and armed, entered bent on thievery. Their targets were a safe stuffed with cash, valuables and gold specimens, and also a wealthy clothier, Charles Levy, who dozed nightly by the stove with his $600-800 bankroll.

Their midnight entry through the hotel's rear door progressed according to plan. But the bandits' furtive approach to the game room was interrupted by an ear-splitting bang. One bungling burglar had accidentally discharged his sawed-off shotgun into the game room ceiling.

Panic hit the robbers. Discovery loomed. With no time to spare, the robbers forgot the safe and ordered the gamesters to line up. Three men leveled guns at the victims, while a fourth relieved hotel owner Robert Foote, along with Ed Brewer and George Ralston, of their gold watches. (Ralston's watch, valued at $500, was a family heirloom.) "I certainly hate to lose that," moaned Foote as the bandit removed his watch. The thief glanced up, and noticed a dazzling $250 diamond stickpin, which Foote had borrowed from friend Charles Moessner to wear for the evening. That, too, disappeared into the robber's pocket. With $50 in cash from the faro bank and bar till, the gang made their get-away, ignoring in their haste the bulging pocketbooks of their victims and the several thousand dollars in the safe.

One of the thieves looked like a real ruffian. Thirty-two year-old Arthur L. Scott, alias Lewis A. Scott, alias J.C. Moore, alias Pug Scott, alias Pug Ryan, displayed a pug nose and a face scarred with a seamy history of barroom brawls and unsavory skirmishes. He stood 5-foot, 6¾ inches, with gray eyes and light hair. Pug Ryan's police "I.D." details a face road-mapped with scars: scar on the right side of neck; small scar on right cheek; small scar on right cheek bone; jaggy scar on left side near eye; scar on outer edge of left eye; large scar on left top of head; two-inch long scar on left side of head; several scars on back of head; right little finger crooked; small scar at base of right thumb; scar on back of left hand; scar on center of knee.

Ryan also had the letters P-U-G tattooed on his arm.

The bandits escaped on foot and scrambled in the dark up and over a steep trail surmounting the Ten Mile Range to Kokomo. There they holed up to sleep in a cabin one mile south of bustling Kokomo, a Ten Mile Canyon mining town.

Irate townspeople of Breckenridge organized. Sheriff Jerry Detwiler, who was serving his first year in office, appointed Breckenridge's Ernest Conrad as deputy. Robert Foote offered Conrad a $100 reward to apprehend the criminals. Conrad boarded the 4 a.m. freight train to Leadville, with plans to travel as far as Kokomo, where a gang of suspicious characters had reportedly taken up residence.

When he arrived at Kokomo, Conrad kept close-mouthed about his mission. A Kokomo newsman asked him whether he came to track the Denver Hotel robbers. Conrad brushed him off with a denial: He had been offered a reward to capture the bandits, but had refused it. He was in Kokomo on personal business. Conrad investigated, and later deputized local resident Sumner Whitney, saloon owner and school board president. About 2 p.m. that Sunday afternoon, August 12, 1898, Conrad and Whitney approached "Robbers Roost".

Inside with the bandits was "Broken Nose Charley", Charles Reilly, a "no-good Kokomo loafer" who, an August 20, 1898 news report said, had rustled "beer and grub for the hungry hyenas". Broken Nose Charley supplied tips to the robbers also, suggesting they hit Leadville's busy Pioneer Saloon the next night.

Conrad had assisted with Breckenridge law enforcement duties for years, but none of that experience prepared him for an encounter with the remorseless Pug Ryan.

A bungled decision would cost the two deputies their lives. Conrad and Whitney surprised Ryan and his men at Robbers Roost. The two law officers had seized the upper hand. But unsure in the face of Ryan's bravado, they concluded that they had made a mistake. Conrad and Whitney apologized and left the cabin.

Once outside, their common sense returned. They re-entered the cabin for a second inspection and demanded: "Boys, we must see what you have got under those blankets."

Suddenly, the scene exploded in gunfire.

Pug Ryan fired his pistol twice with deadly precision. He killed Ernest Conrad with a shot through the head and mortally wounded Sumner Whitney. Whitney managed to shoot bandit Dick Bryant and wound cohort Dick Manley.

What happened to Pug Ryan? He escaped unscathed. But before he bolted, Ryan robbed his wounded partner, Dick Manley, and said, in formal farewell, "God damn you, son-of-a-bitch. I have a notion to kill you." Ryan kicked the defenseless Manley and left.

The bloody shootout at isolated Robbers Roost might easily have gone undetected. But John Barret, a Leadville man standing on a railside platform awaiting the Denver & Rio Grande train heard the shots. He gave the alarm, and Kokomo residents rushed to the scene. First to arrive at the blood-spattered cabin was George Steve, who witnessed Pug Ryan's rifling the dying Manley's pockets. He later testified at Ryan's trial.

Pug Ryan escaped toward Jacque Ridge south of Copper Mountain. Kokomo residents in angry pursuit judged the trail to be "hot" when they found Pug's lighted cigar stump. But they never found Pug.

Citizen leader, father and school board president Sumner Whitney (in white apron), shot in the Robbers Roost gun battle, died after weeks of agony.

Dead lay 42-year old Ernest Conrad, loving husband and father of three young children. He was a respected longtime resident of Breckenridge. Fatally wounded was Sumner Whitney. D. & R. G. conductor Al McCurdy placed his Leadville-bound train at the disposal of Kokomo residents who transported the wounded Whitney to a Leadville hospital. This established Kokomo resident and married father of three children died there on September 7, 1898, less than one month after the shooting. Before he expired, Whitney identified Pug Ryan's photograph. He wrote across it: "This is the man who did the shooting," and signed his name.

Dying robber Dick Manley made a deathbed confession in the Breckenridge jail. It supplied the evidence for an all-points bulletin for Ryan's arrest. Authorities launched a nationwide search for Pug Ryan, with plenty of incentive for the headhunters. The State of Colorado offered a $250 reward for Ryan's capture and conviction. Summit County posted $100 in reward money and El Paso County, also desirous of Pug's return, offered $500. The City of Chicago wanted Pug back for a visit too, with a $1,000 prize for his capture.

The slippery Ryan eluded his captors for four long years. Finally, in April, 1902, Seattle, Washington police picked up a tramp. The scar-faced vagrant protested that he was an innocent Seattle resident, J.C. Moore. But police discovered the letters P-U-G tattooed on his arm and identified the protesting Mr. Moore as murderer Pug Ryan.

An April, 1902 news clip was recently discovered by local Ryan-researcher Peter Fredin in early Denver Detective Sam Howe's scrapbook. It reads:

> Seattle, Wash., April 5. J.C. Moore, alias "Pug" Ryan, alias L.A. Scott, who is wanted in Summit County, Colorado for murder and who is suspected of complicity in the hold-up of a saloon at Franklin, Washington, during which Martin Johnson, bartender, was shot dead, was arrested here last night.

A writ of extradition signed by Washington Governor Henry McBride allowed Breckenridge Sheriff Detwiler and Deputy W.P. Lindsey to pick up Pug Ryan in Seattle and finally return him to Breckenridge for trial.

Detwiler locked Ryan up tight in the Breckenridge jail. But housing a murderer made the sheriff nervous. Would Ryan escape? Besides, keeping a prisoner for an extended jail stay in Breckenridge was expensive. Better to transfer Ryan to the Leadville jail where cheaper rates of $1 per day board prevailed.

Ryan proved a model inmate at Leadville. The sole exception: One Sunday, June 1, 1902, he ungraciously failed to appear at dinner. A trustee serving the sabbath meal noticed that not only Pug, but four other prisoners as well, had sacrificed their Sunday dinner for the lure of freedom.

While the Leadville sheriff was off for an afternoon of fishing, the five fugitives had sawed off a padlock on the sewer trap door and escaped through the watery outlet.

Feeling relaxed, freed from the confining atmosphere of his jail cell, a nostalgic Pug decided to return to his hometown, gold-rich Cripple Creek. There he consulted his attorney, J. Maurice Finn, who tried to persuade Ryan to turn himself in.

The Cripple Creek excursion proved to be a fatal mistake. Night marshal Nicholas Williamson recognized Pug lounging on a street corner at Third and Bennett Saturday night, June 7 around 10 p.m. Williamson promptly arrested the surprised Pug, who claimed to be a vacationing Denverite, Tom Davis, a stationary railroad engineer. But the tattooed P-U-G again provided the giveaway.

All of Breckenridge turned out for Pug Ryan's trial beginning June 14, 1902 at the big G.A.R. (Grand Army of the Republic) Hall, Breckenridge's social center. Ryan played to a packed house—people in Sunday clothes brought lunches to avoid losing a prized court-room seat. Young girls ogled the impenitent felon and swooned, to the shocked dismay of their elders.

The jury couldn't help being moved by Sam Jones' passionate closing plea:

I see a beautiful happy home up Main Street, three young children, a loving mother and a loving husband and father. Suddenly, a mist came over this home. Sam Jones pointed to the defendant and continued, "Oh! Pug Ryan we got you. Four long years but at last. We cannot give you the gallows, but we will give you the nearest to it."

The trial ended Tuesday evening and promptly the next morning, after one hour's deliberation, the jury delivered its verdict: Guilty of murder in the first degree.

Even after Pug Ryan's conviction, Summit County couldn't forget him. A surprising event ten years after the Breckenridge robbery added fuel to the Ryan legend. During the summer of 1908, Allie Carlson and her two cousins, Bertha and Bryan Murrell, picnicked and played on a mountainside near Kokomo. Beside a large log, they discovered the revolver and loot Pug Ryan had buried in a handkerchief there during his escape a decade before. The *Summit County Journal* printed this story:

On Monday afternoon, a bunch of Kokomo children held a luncheon on the summit of Jacque Mountain.

There on the mountainside the Carlson children picked up an old watch and chain. Directly another gold watch was found. Of course the children were excited and naturally ran home with their treasure. (Their father) found the first clue to ownership of one of the watches in the monogram, R.W.F., which it bore.

He called up the Journal by phone and said he had R. W. Foote's and another gold watch and a pearl-handled revolver

and narrated how he came into possession of them.

A morning later Mr. Foote was appraised of the recovery of the forgotten time piece. He took in the situation at once and said, "My diamond is on that hill too; it will be found where the watches were picked up, and I shall take the morning train to Kokomo."

Sunrise next morning found Mr. Foote and Chet Acton knocking at the door of the Carlson home in Kokomo. The children were aroused and they led the way to the lone treasure spot. Acton scratched in the dirt at the spot pointed out by the children and in an instant uncovered the big diamond, to the great joy of him who was ruthlessly deprived of it ten long years before. The second watch proved to be the property of Ed Brewer then residing in Glenwood Springs.

Robert Foote saw his valuable watch restored but recognized that Ernest Conrad and Sumner Whitney could never be restored to their grieving families. When Mrs. Conrad and Mrs. Whitney visited his Denver Hotel three months after the murders in November, 1898,

Foote presented each with a check for $50. A greater remembrance occurred just over a century later when officials added a new wing to the Colorado Law Enforcement Memorial in Washington, D.C. Deputies Conrad and Whitney, who died in the line of duty, had their names and heroic stories added to the assemblage honored at the Memorial.

Oren K. Gaymon, 1899 State Senator, introduced a bill to compensate widows and children of officers slain by Ryan.

Johnny McDaniels, Hooligan

A half-century after gold rush ruffian Pug Ryan came a 1950s hooligan with unusual talents. Now even tiny Heeney, Colorado, located on Green Mountain Reservoir north of Silverthorne, could boast of a resident thug. Johnny McDaniels, the consummate Summit County bad boy, distinguished himself as the criminal who broke out of every American jail, prison and penitentiary he inhabited, including Leavenworth.

McDaniels honed his jailbreaking skills in Summit County where he was arrested and jailed enough times to gain considerable experience. His juvenile and young adult offenses did not rank as small time misdemeanors. By the time he reached maturity McDaniels had faced accusations of:

Murdering his sister's husband
Blowing up the Heeney post office
Firing shots (he missed) with intent to kill the Heeney postmaster
Plotting to kill his niece with a bomb.

The old Frisco calaboose would provide little challenge for jailbreak artist Johnny McDaniels. You can visit this jail at the Frisco Historic Park.

It was a health risk to belong to McDaniels' family. Speaking of his family, one must note that Johnny probably had a rotten childhood. The *Summit County Journal* reported a tragic accident near Green Mountain dam. A Mrs. McDaniels plunged 61 feet to her death while helping her husband work in the McDaniels mine. Six children, ages three to fifteen, survived their mother. A door closed in Johnny McDaniels' life.

Johnny also saw the Summit County jail cell door slam in his face many times for the above-listed youthful indiscretions. This failed to discourage him. He managed to escape almost as often as he was incarcerated.

Naturally Johnny employed explosives in his crimes. He grew up as a miner. Born at the Big Four Mine at Green Mountain, McDaniels learned mining techniques, including handling dynamite. Today people don't think of Heeney and Green Mountain Reservoir area as a mining district but a mineral rush began there around 1903 and mining continued for years. The Bureau of Reclamation constructed Green Mountain dam during World War II around 1942-43.

His talent with explosives and a brilliant engineering mind enabled Johnny to do enormous damage, usually at taxpayer expense. During McDaniels' local heyday in early the 1950s, the county jail occupied a corner of the courthouse basement in Breckenridge. Bored with lounging in jail, the mechanically-gifted inmate once systematically dismantled the jail plumbing system. Next, seeking a less labor-intensive project, he removed the light bulb in his cell and stuck copper pennies into the socket. He blew out the entire courthouse electrical system. Ski pioneer Edna Dercum, who then served as Summit County clerk, had worked late in her office that night. Spooked by the sudden black-out, she scrambled from the building without finishing a job she considered important.

While taking apart the plumbing, McDaniels spied a hefty length of pipe perfect for busting an officer's cranium. He held jailers at bay with the bludgeon demanding that Sheriff Ray Loomis summon the county attorney, Robert Theobald, at once. Loomis quickly yielded to McDaniels' powers of persuasion, as did Theobald, who soon arrived to intervene. The attorney managed to calm a disturbed McDaniels. Jailers quickly installed steel plate in McDaniels' ceiling to thwart further attempts to wreck courthouse utilities.

Steel reinforced ceilings failed to daunt McDaniels. He was also a floor and wall guy. After annihilating the floor in an unsuccessful escape attempt, McDaniels demolished the lathe and plaster wall, only to encounter an impenetrable brick outer wall.

McDaniels had qualities of greatness. He saw failure as a learning step on the route to success. When authorities transferred him back to the Eagle County jail, his prior residence before the Breckenridge jail, officers from Eagle laughed off Sheriff Loomis' gloomy warnings of jailbreak. Eagle, they patiently explained, had just built a state of the art 1950s jail, certainly secure enough to contain a small-timer like McDaniels.

Twenty four hours later radios crackled the news of a major jailbreak at the new Eagle County facility. All the inmates fled except one, a recent arrival who grinned mischievously. "Where are the other guys?" jailers demanded. Johnny McDaniels feigned innocence. "What guys?" he replied.

McDaniels graduated to bigger crimes in bigger places than Summit County. But he came back to Colorado to meet his demise. Susan Donaldson, in *Summit's Courthouse* described the bad decisions that led to his death.

> McDaniels eventually landed in Central City where he got mixed up with an unscrupulous mine promoter. His troubles ended permanently when he became the victim rather than the perpetrator. He and a mine co-worker were shot as they sat in a pickup truck.

His final incarceration insured against the risk of escape. Murderers shoved the two dead bodies into a mine shaft, included the truck, then pushed a Volkswagen on top to secure Summit County's star jailbreaker. In death McDaniels earned the spotlight he always craved. When his ghoulish mine shaft grave was discovered, the McDaniels story made top line Denver newspaper and TV coverage.

Kokomo, Early-Day Hell Hole

In a previous chapter my readers encountered the brazen behavior of claim jumpers whose heinous activities culminated in house jumping. A May, 1880 crowd of 500 Kokomo residents, enraged about house jumping and armed to the teeth, descended on a jumped building and tore the structure to bits, scattering the fragments on the street. My question is, did that really help?

However, this incident adds a link to an unsavory chain of violence, brutality and drunken shootings that established early Kokomo as Summit County's "crime central." Murders in Kokomo far outranked similar thuggery in Breckenridge and Frisco. Quiet Dillon didn't compare.

Kokomo's history began at its spring, 1879 founding with robbery. Road agents frequented the muddy morass of a road over Fremont Pass and in May of 1879 a band of robbers held up a freight wagon. As late as 1883, the road hadn't improved. Captain John W. Jacque, a prominent mining man, faced off road agents near Kokomo. They startled his horse who reared and threw Jacque to the rocky ground where he lay unconscious. The thieves, possibly undesirables hired by the railroad contractors, robbed his limp body and escaped.

Alcohol fueled much of the violence that marred the otherwise lively history of the Upper Ten Mile Canyon. At the flourishing town of Robinson, Kokomo's neighbor, drunken shootouts endangered the lives not only of the pistol-waving gunmen but innocent bystanders. A little girl narrowly escaped death when a saloon altercation ended with inebriated combatants emptying their six guns at close range. Bullets grazed the child. After Colorado Lt. Governor Robinson died of a gunshot wound in his Robinson Mine, his dignified mother, Mrs. Forbes, came west to oversee his estate. Trigger-happy guards at the mine nearby her lodging, the Robinson Hotel, launched a ten-minute fusillade of gunfire that blew bedposts and lamps away—and nearly blew Mrs. Forbes away as well.

Shattered bedposts would fail to faze Kokomo residents who witnessed frequent alcohol-incited gun battles. One observer noted one to twenty gunshots fired there every night. The *Summit County Journal*'s Kokomo correspondent as late as August, 1894, when Kokomo crime had diminished, called the average man on the street a "walking arsenal." A decade earlier, bullets erupted at the slightest prompting. The job of Kokomo magistrate probably required having an obituary written and ready for publication.

In 1880 Charley Norton, then the proprietor of Breckenridge's Senate Saloon, and his crony Patsy Thorton got drunk in Kokomo. Pals Norton and Thornton, enraged with another bar patron, threatened to lynch the man. This writer has come across reports that a mob did hang the fellow but authors Dempsey and Fell in their *Mining the Summit* document these reports as just persistent rumors.

Another devilish duo, one of them an ex-Kokomo marshal, drank themselves into a violent mood in the next year, in June, 1881. Al Huggins, a thug of bad repute, and the former policeman, Phillip Foote, began shooting up a saloon. Then the hooligan Huggins spied Kokomo mayor Donald Doncaster. Huggins swung his gun's business end toward the mayor. Happily he missed.

This act caught the attention of a police office, the popular Thomas Brown, who intervened with an attempt to calm Huggins. Huggins first loosed a barrage of curses on Brown, then followed up with bullets. Brown, hit in the chest, sank to the ground. The drunken malevolents realized their need to escape and fled to the neighboring town of Recen. Backed by a hastily-assembled posse, Marshal Sutton pursued the drunkards there. When Huggins resisted arrest, he was shot in the face with a shotgun but not mortally wounded.

*A rare photograph shows both Kokomo-Recen in the foreground and brief
(1879-81) Carbonateville in the background, below the hills. Drunkenness,
violence, robbery and claim-jumping flourished in Kokomo's early days.*

Lynching fever arose in outrage over the beloved Brown's shooting, so Sutton shoved his prisoners onto a train bound for Leadville and its jailhouse. In the confusion, Phillip Foote escaped from the train. Felon's luck prevailed for the depraved Huggins. Brown did not die as expected, so Huggins faced charges only for assault and battery with intent to kill.

The next violent year, in October, 1882, a Kokomo man named Marshall shot a man named Moran. Two months later a miner and saloon inmate had a lively discussion using bullets instead of conversation. The *Breckenridge Daily Journal* jeered, "Nice place, this Kokomo!"

A murderous August, 1884 explosives artist tried to blow up P.Y. Thomas' mercantile as the owner and his family slept in residential quarters inside the store. The miscreant detonated a blast outside the store which blew out the front windows. The demented arsonist expected the first blast to explode another stash of powder hidden inside the premises. The second blast failed but the *Journal* railed at the attempt, calling it "the most dastardly outrage ever perpetrated in a civilized town."

Civilized?

TEN: *Watering Holes*

omfortable names like Miners Home Saloon, Miners Rest and Angels Rest evoke images of snug havens, sanctuaries from dulling toil and hospitable retreats. The saloon indeed supplied these comforts to the all-male population of early 1860s Colorado placer mining camps. In what eyewitness Daniel Conner called "a motley assortment of strangers," the mostly-young men far from families and sweethearts found solace in new friends, a free lunch and a genial barkeep.

Saloons

Other early saloon services included a locked safe to secure a pouch of gold dust, a place to vote in an early-day election and a hastily-assembled courtroom to dispense Miners Court justice. The saloon also provided a pulpit for gospel preachers like Methodist Snow Shoe Itinerant John Lewis Dyer. The Victorian mindset tolerated combining the sacred and the base, as long as the arrangement wore the right façade. A blanket tossed over the bar and a discreet

cover for any voluptuous nude paint-
ings transformed the saloon into a
respectable preaching house.

The miners observed the Sabbath
rest, leaving their labors behind—not
to attend church—but to resort to the
genial mine camp whiskey joint. Since
Sunday supplied bars their best
income of the week, preaching there
took place on Saturday or a weekday,
a practical solution to satisfy both
God and money. Frustrated ministers
who viewed music as sinful often had
to wait for fiddlers or a bawdy theatrical troupe to finish, then preach to a
bleary-eyed but properly solemn, hat-
in-hand, congregation.

*Fr. Dyer used a saloon pulpit to preach
against gambling, drinking, fiddling
and dancing.*

British poet Lord Byron turned
his distinguished pen to light verse when he wrote,

> *Let us have wine and women, mirth and laughter.*
> *Sermons and soda water the day after.*

The original saloon ideal with its hosting of public meetings,
church and mine district justice didn't last long. What a sacrilege that
the miners' sanctuary saw its hospitality invaded by a disorderly
sporting element, a debauched bunch of revelers with everything
from mischief to villainy on their minds.

Many who scrambled over the Divide to the gold fields and silver camps were escapees from Eastern society. Father Rhabanus
Gutmann, the portly pastor of St. Mary's Catholic Church in 1880s

Breckenridge, was disgusted at uncivilized Summit County. Not only did he regard his rectory "cold as a dog kennel" but he frowned upon the camp's sporting element. He complained, "It seems as if all the roustabouts, rascals, loose women, adulterers etc find their way to Breckenridge."

William Byers, who founded the *Rocky Mountain News,* traveled through the Blue River valley in 1861 and remarked that "Loafing and gambling are assiduously patronized." He observed " a half dozen sporting saloons are regularly open, day and night."

True, idlers, loafers, bums and wastrels formed a high percentage of the mine camp population. These men lounged in saloons, wasting their days. At night they enjoyed the convenience of the saloon as a flop house. A bar boy at closing time chalk-marked the rough plank floor into rectangles, each barely large enough to accommodate a boozehound's body. Fifty cents bought a place to sleep and a rolled-up coat provided a pillow. (If a pickled patron hit the floor before bedtime due to passing out, he was said to "bite the dust," that is bite the filthy sawdust of the barroom floor, which was probably an unspeakable place for sweet repose.)

Upon awakening the sleeper found the convenience of an eye-opener close at hand. A wag once suggested, "The only real cure for a hangover is death." A less cynical sage remarked, "I feel sorry for people who don't drink. When they get up in the morning, that is as good as they are going to feel."

How bad the intemperate felt the morning after resulted from the toxic ingredients of mine camp whiskey as well as its alcoholic content. To stretch the contents of the whiskey barrel bartenders added tobacco, red pepper, lye and other dangerous chemicals. Others put a less malevolent mix of water and burnt sugar to create "brandy." Taos white lightnin' got its name from the near-lethal electrifying reaction it caused in consumers.

Spittoons, a brass rail, gambling machines and gaming tables in the rear were saloon standards. The burro in the Senate Saloon? Maybe not.

Abstainer Horace Greeley, Greeley, Colorado founder, commented, "I have not tasted it but the smell I can not escape and I am sure a more wholesome potable might be compounded of spirits of turpentine, *aqua fortis* and steeped tobacco. Its look alone will condemn it—soapy, ropy, turbid, it is within bounds to say that every part of it contains as much poison as a gallon of pure whiskey."

Not all whiskey parlors served rotgut and turned into flop houses in the wee hours. Some saloons doubled as real inns for the hundreds of travelers arriving daily in the frenzied mine camps. A saloon downstairs with a sleeping room upstairs challenged the tipsy only with negotiating a steep stairway.

Sleep presented another challenge. Wood boxes stuffed with lodgepole pine boughs and covered with rough muslin jammed into a room marked with a sign, No More Than Five in a Bed. Lice, smelly wet socks, snoring and the evil red eyes of pack rats made slumber elusive. One wayfarer left a Kremmling alehouse early and climbed the stairs to get a good bunk. Those carousing in the saloon could not fail to hear a volley of gunfire some time later. Racing up the stairs expecting to see dead bodies they encountered instead a sheepish guest surrounded by walls and ceiling riddled with bullet holes. He looked at his smoking gun. "Bed bugs," he explained. "I was shooting the bed bugs."

More deadly gunfire often erupted in barrooms. The Leadville daily published a column headlined "Breakfast Bullets," which listed the names of those killed in violent shootings the day before.

Frisco could have published the same after the night of October 20, 1881 when James McWalters, a British bartender at Morrow's Saloon, got feisty with some Irish gamblers and ended up bludgeoned and stabbed on a saloon's sawdusty floorboards. McWalters finished his shift at 9:15 and headed for another saloon, Isadoor Smith's, where he got into a card game and consumed undetermined amounts of whiskey and blackberry brandy, according to the November 5, 1881 *Colorado Weekly Republican.* The other gamblers, James Driscoll and Patrick Hopkins, accused McWalters of cheating. To this the Brit responded with a barrage of obscene curses and a lunge for the saloon's rifle above the bar. Driscoll grabbed a pistol and using its butt delivered McWalters a skull-crushing blow to the head. A knife finished the argument, and McWalters as well.

An inquest lasting two and one-half days followed. Both police justice Henry Learned and the six-man jury needed a strong collective stomach because the corpse of the victim lay stretched out on the barroom floor during the entire deliberation.

Despite sordid happenings, mine towns boasted about their numbers of saloons as sign of prosperity, according to Robert L. Brown in his *Saloons of the American West*. He writes that Kokomo, in Summit County's Ten Mile Canyon below Fremont Pass, "bragged that it had 100 operating saloons along Ten Mile Avenue in 1881." Though this figure is a wild exaggeration—probably liquor talking— it shows the esteem held for saloons. Their proprietors held the same prominence as the assayer, banker and physician. Saloon owners enjoyed prosperity, proving the observation, "The only way to get ahead is to sell liquor—or to drink it." Breckenridge had 18 saloons and three dance halls at the very onset of the 1879-80 hardrock mining rush. Dr. Arthur V. Garretson who visited the town as a wide-eyed ten year old in the early 1880s said he saw "a saloon or gambling house at every other door."

The mine town's pride in its saloons combined with the happy prospect of receipts from license fees imposed on saloon owners. Fees brought about $300 per year per saloon into Breckenridge town coffers, the mainstay of many town budgets. Frisco saloons each paid their town $250 yearly in 1884. Later fees rose. Around 1900 Kokomo each saloon paid $300 for six months.

Financial successes enabled saloons to evolve with the growing wealth of the town. Early camps housed saloons in tents and rough log shanties. A board laid across two whiskey barrels served as a bar. Placer mining profits allowed proprietors to upgrade their drinking houses' architecture to sawn-board buildings. When the lode boom detonated in 1879-80, population soared and Victorian false-front structures embellished with gingerbread began to line local main streets. Hurdy gurdy houses upgraded their structures, building new Victorian frame edifices.

An old log saloon stood on the northwest corner of Lincoln and Main in Breckenridge in 1888 that demonstrates this trend. John B.

Dewers, proprietor of the Corner Saloon contracted in January, 1888 to build a new 26x80 foot saloon there with office space upstairs. "When completed it will be the most commodious saloon, billiard hall and club rooms in town," an approving January 31, 1888 *Summit County Journal* declared. (For the story of John Dewers' tragic death in a love triangle, see page 108.)

Barrooms in elegant 1880s hotels began to attract well-dressed gents with pomaded moustaches. But the thin veneer of mine town respectability scratched easily. In 1885 a dozing drunk awoke in a stupor and grabbed two chairs swinging them in the air and "jabbering in an unknown tongue," according to the *Journal.* When an ornate chandelier crashed down on the crowd, the marshal was summoned. In another scratch on the thin veneer of respectability, a group of well-dressed gents were relieved of their gold watches and diamonds in 1898 by Pug Ryan and his gang of thugs. They invaded Breckenridge's fashionable Denver Hotel to line up imbibers at gunpoint and take their treasures. While the Victorian Denver Hotel structure is now as absent as were the gentlemen's watches, its historic Brunswick bar, crafted from mahogany in Brunswick, Maine and its diamond dust mirror resides in the Horseshoe II restaurant.

Less elegant, the saloons in Montezuma still managed to indulge their overalls-and-hobnail-boot clad clientele. Everett Hugh Brines as a boy cleaned and polished brass spittoons in his father's saloon daily. Later each morning he trudged uphill a quarter mile to get the daily ice supply. An old mine tunnel on the mountainside had ice in it year round. Everett toted a gunnysack of ice he had hewed from the frozen mass back to the bar so patrons could enjoy cold drinks.

Several saloon businesses survived from gold rush days and today still refresh the dry and the weary. These historic saloons include:

The Mint, 341 Blue River Parkway, Silverthorne: An early Summit County resident, Jimmy Ryan established the Mint in 1880s Dillon, the original town site now submerged beneath Lake Dillon. Some say the building saw its first light in the Ten Mile Canyon silver camp of Kokomo, then moved to Frisco in 1879 and Dillon in 1882. In Old Dillon, the Mint, located on Main Street near Rudolph Kremmling's general store, served ranchers, miners and town residents.

The Old Dillon Inn, 321 Blue River Parkway, Silverthorne: Again, some say this building began in 1879 in another town, Frisco, then moved to Old Dillon to become a bar. Old timers disagree. They agree, however, that the original tavern had only the barroom and pool table room in the rear. In the early 1940s the Old Dillon Inn building housed four separate enterprises: the small bar with tables in the back; the postoffice operated by Ira Blundell; an apartment occupied by Frank and Katherine Valaer Warren; and a coffee shop with a few groceries run by a couple from Green Mountain, where the new dam was being built. Minnie and Eric Erickson ran the 1940s ODI which sat next door to the Dillon Garage.

Longtime Dillon residents don't like their town portrayed as a rough place but one story from a woman who lived there, Sena Valaer, documents a real crime that occurred in the 1950s at the Old Dillon Inn. Here is the story:

Mrs. Virgil Cox, a saloon-owner's wife in Old Dillon, waited for her husband's late arrival home. He always closed the bar at 2 a.m., locked up and walked across the street to his house and she always watched for him.

Despite having eight saloons and liquor establishments for just 80 residents, Dillon was a pretty safe town. Vera Cox had never needed to worry.

Old Dillon Inn (left), located in early town now beneath the Dillon Reservoir, today operates in Silverthorne. Its 1950s holdup story hasn't been told till now.

That night her Virgil didn't come home. Mrs. Cox put on a coat and negotiated the dark crossing to peer in the bar window. She blinked as horror invaded her mind. The cash register stood open. An unsavory-looking man had a gun to Virgil's head as he sat at a table, his arms crossed.

Adrenalin pumping, Mrs. Cox ran home to telephone police.

The local constable, J. Ross, hung up the phone and yawned wearily. Grumbling, he got dressed and headed out into the cold night air. *Women and their big imaginations,* he muttered. If he wanted to keep his job, he'd have to check it out.

Just what he thought. Looking into the saloon window, the policeman observed Virgil Cox, his arms on the table, with a companion. *Just having a whiskey and some conversation,* the constable allowed. He considered going on back to bed.

Better just bang on the door to show I was here doing my job, he cautioned himself. He tried the door. Locked, as it should be after 2 a.m. He yelled "Hey, Virgil," and pounded.

Inside R. Sides, an ex-con who had come to the Dillon area to work on the Roberts Tunnel Denver water diversion project, panicked. Virgil Cox seized the opportunity. "We've got to let him in," he warned.

With the robber's gun trained on him, Virgil unlocked the door. "Watch out," he whispered to Ross. The officer offered an apologetic grin. "Sorry boys, just doing my job. Won't bother you long because —" Shots rang out. (The blast woke Sena Valaer who later related this story.) The startled officer fumbled for his gun as the thug shouted "Throw the gun on the sidewalk."

Cox and the constable were held at bay while the felon raced for an approaching car. When an accomplice, his brother, pulled up, Sides still brandished the cop's gun. He noticed Vera Cox, who had come back out, hiding behind a car and forced her into the bar. Just then a semi-truck driver who had parked on the street noticed that the bar was open and strolled over for a late night nip. The surprised truck driver was herded into the bar as well. This disruption allowed officer J. Ross to slip away, circle the building and retrieve a second gun from the town hall. But the returned to find only a cloud of dust.

The thugs' car roared away in the direction of Loveland Pass. A shaky Ross telephoned the State Patrol to apprehend the pair. The phone rang and rang; no state Patrol officer was on duty. The ex-cons got away. And the Coxes got little sleep that night.

Later the Sides brothers attempted a crime in Denver and this time R. Sides was killed. One of the hooligans still carried the Dillon policeman's gun, identified by its serial numbers.

Bubba's Bones Barbeque/Angels Rest, 110 South Ridge Street, Breckenridge. Fr. John L. Dyer's idyllic retreat at timberline near Boreas Pass railroad route had its tranquility shattered when Jerry Krigbaum relocated the Angels Rest saloon there. Fr. Dyer believed liquor came straight from the devil and said so. Fr. Dyer had retired at his new-founded Dyersville to get away from raucous Breckenridge. Needless to say, his wrath rested on Jerry Krigbaum.

Krigbaum ignored Dyer's ire, as a July 27 *Breckenridge Daily Journal* article suggests:

> Angels Rest is a point near the top of the divide which some say is as near heaven as many of the angels would ever get; and as may be of a mixed kind, Father Dyer attends to the spiritual needs of the heavenly inclined, while Jerry Krigbaum applies the spirituous stimulants of the other sorts. Wicked passerbys say that Jerry has the most calls.

Krigbaum earned local favor because he treated his clientele to an extravaganza Christmas dinner. He made two holiday trips to Breckenridge in his two-horse sleigh to load up a ten gallon keg of whiskey, oysters, turkey, eggs, cranberries and trimmings.

The date when the Angels Rest closed its doors in Dyersville is unknown but remnants of the restaurant-saloon remain at the site. (See the author's book, *The New Summit Hiker* for the Indiana Creek Trail to Dyersville.) In 1973 Paul Mahoney opened a 3.2 bar on Ridge Street and called it the Angels Rest.

The resurrected bar occupied an 1880s cabin once used by L.L. Hilliard to assay Colorado's heftiest gold nugget. Named Tom's Baby for its 1887 discoverer Tom Groves, the spectacular gold hunk was first weighed here in the privacy of Hilliard's living room, even though his assay office stood right across the street. Tom toted his

13 pound, 7 ounce troy weight "baby" around town in a blanket to show off the find. In recent years Bubbas Bones Barbeque opened in that same building.

The Historic Brown Hotel Restaurant, 208 North Ridge Street, Breckenridge. Tom and Maude Brown expanded a primitive hewn-log 1880s structure in 1898 and laughingly named their new hotel after both the luxurious Brown Palace in Denver and themselves. The Brown Hotel installed the first bathtub in Summit County. Captain Brown, a Britisher, took full advantage of this innovation by advertising it heavily. His ads also promised the hotel "very respectable and safe for maiden ladies." Brown's wife, the personable Maude, probably attracted more guests than the advertisements and gave her favorite guests the best room in the house, the warm one over the kitchen and its woodstove.

Earlier the Brown Hotel had housed Captain and Mrs. Ryan. He owned French Gulch's prosperous Oro Mine in partnership with black pioneer Barney Ford. She ran a school in her home at the hotel, which made education convenient for the couple's two young sons. After the Oro's sale to prominent townsmen who merged it with the Wellington Mine, the Ryans sold their home.

Throughout its history, including the Depression years, the Brown Hotel has never closed.

The Gold Pan, 103 North Main Street, Breckenridge. Grand claims about the Gold Pan's history included an 1983 bar manager statement that the bar was 122 years old that year and "the oldest continuously operating bar west of the Mississippi." While that's quite a boast, the Gold Pan can demand respect as the oldest operating bar in Summit County and one of Colorado's oldest.

Its age verified by the tipsy condition of its building, the Gold

Pan combines two drunken clapboard buildings leaning on one another. Their aging foundations, on their eay to delirium tremens, are of ancient log. The two-building combination paid off when fire threatened to demolish both. Firemen pulled the south structure away from the north and saved today's Gold Pan.

The Gold Pan never caved in to Prohibition when it was Bradley's Saloon. The thirsty could always sneak a drink in Bradley's back room. And the Gold Pan never caved in to the pressure to become a cutsey ski town bar. Its plain-facts interior has a bit of a rough look and its patrons don't wear designer jeans.

On the other hand, its historic bar has real class. Brunswick artisans crafted its egg and dart trim bar. Legend says the bar arrived by mule train from Leadville where it served another Breckenridge saloon until 1920. Ionic columns frame the bar's massive mirror.

People say that an 1861 watering hole, Long's Saloon, stood on the site. Later it became the Palace, a restaurant-bar with an aquarium in the front window. Customers could select their own trout for dinner. The three Bradley brothers ran their bowling alley there during Prohibition. The Gold Pan is reputed to have had a tunnel from the bar underneath Main Street to a bunk house across the way.

Colorado saloon historian Tom Noel, in his *Liquid History,* says that a bar has occupied the site paying local taxes since 1865, although the first section of the present building was built in 1879 for the Herman Strauss saloon. The structure housed a bowling alley around 1910 and later Bradley's Saloon. Tom Noel records a funeral parlor operated on the site but local historians dispute this.

Breckenridge's last saloon gunfight erupted in the Gold Pan in the early 1960s. The Breckenridge Ski Area had opened in 1961 and workers often ended the day in the Gold Pan. When voices heated in argument began to rise, customers watched as one of the dissenters, an Hispanic man who had played the bowling machines, got up and strode out the door. He hurried to town marshal Bob Brown's apartment upstairs in the old Hilliard-Angels Rest building and grabbed Brown's assault rifle. Returning to the Gold Pan he stationed himself in Main Street and opened fire into he bar. A bullet struck a woman using the telephone in the hip, causing serious injury.

Everyone smoked back then and the health damage was outweighed that day by smoking's one advantage: Ted Nickerson took a bullet to the heart. But he had a Zippo metal cigarette lighter in his breast pocket that deflected the bullet and saved his life.

Moonshiners

Colorado's saloon era, birthed into lusty vigor at the onset of the 1859 gold rush, halted forever January 1, 1916 when state prohibition law took effect. Almost immediately, Colorado's remote gulches and mountain mine tunnels sprouted with moonshiners. The state's roadways, hacked out for stagecoaches and ore transport, flowed with new traffic generated by bootleggers. Summit County moonshiners set up stills in Laskey Gulch, on Mt. Royal and down the Blue. Transformed saloons like Bradleys (now the Gold Pan) allowed a preferred clientele access to a secret back room where liquor and cigars soothed patrons troubled by temperance.

The temperance movement began in the 1850s when outrage arose over drunken husbands, abused wives and deprived children. An intense nationwide campaign was mounted by the 1874-founded

Women's Christian Temperance Union (WCTU) and the 1893-forged Anti-Saloon League, which consolidated efforts of the Methodist, Baptist, Congregational and Presbyterian churches. Temperance speakers painted a lurid picture of the evils of saloon life. When prohibition finally ended in 1933, repealed by the Constitution's twenty-first amendment, the institution of the all-male saloon labored under a negative image so irreversible that it died. Cocktail lounges and bars replaced that bastion of male comfort and release from drudgery. The saloon disappeared from the American cultural scene.

A sorrowful Christopher Morley took a pen to his grief:

The earth is grown puny and pallid,
The earth is grown gouty and grey,
For whiskey is no longer valid
And wine has been voted away.
As for beer, we will no longer swill it
In riotous, rollicking spree.
The little hot dogs on the skillet
Will have to be swallowed with tea.

Prohibition gave impetus to the Roaring Twenties when bootlegging, smuggling, speakeasies, blind pig joints, rumrunning and moonshining ran rampant. It resulted in a new demand from women to drink alongside men. Prohibition also gave rise to crime organizations such as the mafia who competed often in violent ways for the illicit liquor trade.

Another nationwide result, this one amusing, involved getaway cars. When a unit of the Internal Revenue Service chased a bootlegger, the enforcers often could not outrun the booze runners who souped up their 1920s buggies with additional horsepower and, yes, turbo chargers. America's moonshiners became top-notch mechanics

A cabin high on Mt. Royal with a whiskey still hidden in the brush behind made a scenic and secluded brewery for producing white lightnin' moonshine.

and the bootleggers became expert race car drivers. The best ended up in the new sport of NASCAR racing. One early NASCAR driver remarked, "The fastest car I ever drove was a bootleg car."

Revenuers rarely made it to Summit County where local moonshine kept the populace merry-hearted. But high altitude moonshine cookery proved challenging. At sea level the grain or corn mash for white lightning needed to cook at exactly 172 degrees. At that temperature the mash would not boil but the alcohol would convert to steam. Getting the recipe right at 9,000 to 10,000 feet where water boils low was as tricky for moonshiners as baking an angel food cake was for housewives. After a "worm" process where the alcohol condensed back to a liquid with the help of cold water (no lack there), the moonshine was strained and jugged. Moonshine is usually 100 proof

A copper still used for moonshine displayed in historic Frisco jail.

(50 percent alcohol). Because moonshiners do not age their liquor in oak barrels like whiskey it is not amber in color. It is clear, or white, thus the name white lightning.

The miners knew how to check the alcohol content of local moonshine. They poured the liquor onto gun powder then lit the mixture. They probably yelled "fire in the hole" and backed off fast. If the moonshine ignited, it was declared worthy of consumption.

For ranchers in Summit County's Lower Blue valley the opportunity to be finicky about moonshine was limited since its availability was likewise limited. Some ranchers were forced to live on nothing but food and water! The still at the old town of Naomi where Rock Creek meets the Blue River produced the only local "mountain dew." Frances Long of Acorn Creek Ranch loves to tell this story about a local moonshiner named Kennedy:

Kennedy's liquor is reputed to have killed a sick calf whose owner administered the stuff as medicine. But the spirits did not finish off Mrs. Long's well-known grandfather, horseman and rancher Thomas Alva Marshall. "My grand-dad had been terribly sick. The doctor suggesting getting bootlegger Kennedy's whiskey to use as a stimulant. The sick Marshall drank the moonshine and rallied. Upon hearing this news, Kennedy, a born marketer, had labels printed up touting his moonshine as "doctor recommended."

With the right wind, the sheriff could smell the sweet tang of mash like that cooked at Naomi a long way off. Noisy burners could also tip off authorities. Whiskey stills, kettles, tubs and copper cables weren't easy to hide. (Smoke from the still fire could be piped into a cabin and emerge from the kitchen chimney looking like harmless cooking smoke.)

Moonshiners around Frisco on Mt. Royal had it easier. They could hide their operations in mine tunnels. White Mule, Blue John, Purple Jesus, Sneaky Peter, cow whiskey or scorpion juice, whatever you called it, could be hidden away in a mine tunnel high on a steep slope with little chance of discovery. Once however a hungry mule led authorities to a still. When they found the mule hitched to a post at an empty cabin, a deputy untied the mule and followed him up a thickly forested side canyon to a shack where the hungry animal stuck his nose deep in a pile of warm sour mash. The concealed still stood a few feet away.

When time came to transport the illegal ambrosia from these secret stills, the bootlegger stepped onto the scene.

Bootleggers

The term bootlegging evokes images of backwoods Kentucky. The word saw its origin, however, in the West where fur traders' forts and later gold rush settlers brewed their beverages and carried their bottles to buyers stowed in the loose top of their knee-high boots.

Bootleggers sold their liquid wares to Summit County bars that had in 1916 turned into mock billiard halls, bowling alleys or restaurants. The liquored traveled to these false-fronted "fronts" in creative vehicles as unusual as a hearse or as mundane as a hay wagon.

Gents delivering moonshine to a speakeasy relied on cars that ran, and ran fast.

One pundit wrote,

> *Hush little saloon, don't you cry*
> *You'll be a drugstore by and by.*

About 20 minutes after prohibition ended with repeal in 1933 , Summit County bars threw open their doors in joyous glee.

Had they foreseen the inevitable outcome, Summit newspaper editors might not have showcased temperance speakers. Speakers Miss White and Miss DeVelling gave well-promoted 1887 temperance lectures in Breckenridge. One local saloon keeper, Scott McClarren, got so caught up in the oratory that he took the pledge— for ten years! (Then McClarren upped and died, proving forever the ill-effects of abstinence.)

Commodore Stephen Decatur who founded his namesake mine camp, Decatur, in Summit's Peru Creek valley near Montezuma, deliv-

Pomaded hair, striped tie and suit, plus a cigar, flaunt the new-found wealth of the bootlegger making a deal during Prohibition.

ered stirring orations on temperance, moving many to take the pledge. Decatur himself was a secret tippler and later died of alcoholism.

The temperance movement and the prohibition it produced so smeared the saloon that bars, clubrooms and cocktail lounges, now the province of both men and women, replaced the male bastion of the saloon.

Those who still miss the old Western saloon will find inspiration in this verse by Don Marquis from "The Old Brass Railing:"

> *Myself, I can endure the drouth*
> *With stoic calm, and prayer.*
> *But my feet still seek a railing*
> *When a railing isn't there.*

1910 Postcard.

Eleven: *Frontier Justice*

T his book's miserable collection of blighters, cads, bounders and thugs throughout the decades of the gold rush mostly got away with their misbegotten behavior. They would never have possessed the nerve to commit their crimes had Judge Marshall Silverthorn remained on duty. As judge of the miners court in early 1860s Breckenridge, the wiry bantam rooster of a man dispensed justice with a swift and sure hand.

Judge Silverthorn and the Miners Court

The noose lay ready when a public enemy arrived at the miners court for judgment. Prospectors modeled this no-red-tape judicial forum after miners courts in the 1849 California gold rush. Four categories of offense—murder, theft, claim-jumping and skullduggery—existed. If the infraction didn't equal murder, theft or claim-jumping, it certainly fell under the intentionally-vague category of skullduggery. (If you go to the dictionary to find this word, you'll be disappointed. Trust me, the miners clumped all kinds of villainous behavior into the catch-all of "skullduggery.")

Like frontier justice around the American West, prompt retribution followed on the heels of a crime in 1860s Breckenridge, Montezuma and the Ten Mile Canyon. A ruffian could rob a U.S. mail carrier at 6 a.m., have a price on his hooligan head at 7 a.m., be arrested and tried by the miners court by 2 p.m., be hung and have his corpse keep an appointment with the coroner before 3. With the reward money paid out, the felon's funeral could finish before celebratory whiskey was poured out in a tent saloon that same day at sunset.

John Young, who visited Summit County's Blue River Diggings in 1860 reported his memoir *John D. Young and the Colorado Gold Rush* his first-hand observation of a California Gulch miners court in action:

> If there was any dispute about the title of a claim it was decided by miners' meeting . . . a trial would go on just the same as in any court of justice . . . After the testimony a vote would be taken "viva voce" and that decision would be final. If the defeated party insisted on holing your claim after that . . . you would be justified in shooting him dead.
>
> It was the same for any criminal offense murder, horse stealing, stealing . . . For lesser offenses the punishment was a number of lashes laid on the bare back and the prisoner tied to a tree . . . the prisoner was banished and on pain of death ever to show himself again in the community. Among so many turbulent spirited, all the desperadoes from the states, you may be sure that scarcely a night passes that some one or more was on trial and capital punishment was of frequent occurrence.

Vigilante justice and public lynching certainly occurred in Colorado, especially in early-day Denver. But in Summit County, like other mining regions, the miners court meted out punishment for crime. Prospectors formed a mining district as soon as a camp sprang up and usually established trial procedures. While some had no permanent officers, wrote no laws and kept no records, Summit County mining districts drew up bylaws and kept meeting records. Judge Silverthorne kept district records in his 1861-established Silverthorn Hotel. County documents show payment for judicial service made to Silverthorn on April 1, 1862. The amount: $1.

Ironically, the man who spearheaded the first mining district in Summit County's Ten Mile Canyon was named Justice—Henry C. Justice. On Monday, August 21, 1860 prospectors assembled on Fremont Pass near gold-rich McNulty Gulch to draw up laws and establish officers and rules for the governance of the district. Henry Justice immediately afterward discovered the Ten Mile's first silver lode. Prospectors rushed to the site and the district's first claim dispute erupted. Henry Justice and Hugh Strickland, district president, resolved the clash using the Ten Mile district's new laws.

As was the typical arrangement, a jury of six claim-owning miners decided on all trials in the new Ten Mile district. The miners court there gave right of appeal to the "justice court of the Blue River judicial district"—and Breckenridge's feisty Judge Silverthorn.

No such appeal occurred in the case of Montezuma's Red Mike. A kangaroo court, not a miners court, determined his ugly fate. Three prominent Montezuma businessmen regularly accompanied Irishman Red Mike on their freight haul over Webster Pass to the town of Webster in Handcart Gulch. The men, who camped overnight before their return to Montezuma, always brought plenty of liquor to accompany their campsite poker games.

Judge Silverthorn's miners court retained power to hang offenders. "Judge Lynch" also ruled, with most lynching in places with no mine district laws.

During one overnight in 1879 Mike got drunk and ornery. The other three, as drunk as Mike, held a kangaroo court and voted to hang the belligerent Irishman. They dragged him to a tree where they looped the noose and strung him up. The trio planned to give him a few moments of scare, then cut him down. But a challenging poker hand caused them a fatal distraction. Mike strangled.

Next morning, sobered up, the horrified men saw Mike dangling. They turned his horses loose and made a liars' pact to say that Mike had left them in Webster. When travelers discovered his body they concluded the death occurred during a robbery. The true story failed to emerge for decades.

Back in Breckenridge, the Judge presided over a formal court week each year. Court week quickly became an excuse for a big party. Fiddlers, accompanied by an organ, played music for the annual dance. When court week was not in session the judge carried out justice on an as-needed basis.

Need arose regularly including one 1860s day in Breckenridge. The judge though tiny as a leprechaun took on the biggest bullies. He noticed a drunk misbehaving on Breckenridge streets. He himself made out a warrant and served it on the inebriate. Then he seized the prisoner by the back of the neck and kicked him up the side of the hill to lock him up in the town calaboose—all this on a day the Judge has complained of feeling ill.

Strong arm tactics like those of Judge Silverthorn, undertaken before the Miranda law and offenders' rights decisions, were administered by a tiny shriveled up miniature of a judge. In today's world, his aggressive physical methods would incite a protest. But remember that 1860s Breckenridge earned the label of "a fiendish place" and its population earned the description "a motley group of rough individuals." In the author's book *SUMMIT, A Gold Rush History of Summit*

County, Colorado, this 1883 description of Judge Silverthorn by the
grandiose traveling authoress Alice
Polk Hill appears:

> He is a diminutive man, almost
> dried to a crackling, and has such a
> strange, weird look . . . His hair and
> beard are grizzly gray, and he
> chews continually. When he tells a
> border tale his little keen eyes twin-
> kle with humor and intelligence,
> then he goes into convulsions of
> laughter and kicks up his feet until
> he resembles a jack-knife half
> open—forming a picture alto-
> gether grotesque. But he is the soul
> of honor and goodness, with a heart so large that it is contin-
> ually running over with kind deeds and comforting words.

Old Judge Marshal Silverthorn

More stories of kindness demonstrated by both Judge Silverthorn
and his well-loved wife, Agnes exist than stories of tough frontier justice. The fact remains, however, that Summit County's colorful
parade of sinners—polecats, rotters, knaves and blackguards—may
never have marched across the Summit County scene if Judge Silverthorn and his ilk stayed in charge.

Happily, his justice didn't last forever. We had a bounty of rogues
and villains. They left us plenty to laugh about in our larger-than-life
gold rush history.

Victorian Names for No Goods

Swindler
- double dealer
- cheat
- swindler
- defrauder
- blackleg (a gambling cheat)
- crook
- sneak
- charlatan
- mountebank (originally one who mounted a bench to sell quack medicines)
- trickster
- prevaricator (literally "to walk crookedly;" liar)
- fabricator (liar)
- jackdaw in peacock feathers (a jackdaw is a small crow)
- double dealer
- four flusher
- Judas

Lawyer
- shyster (unethical lawyer)
- pettifogger (handles petty or trumped up cases)

Faker
- imposter
- poseur (imposter, fake)
- sham (trickster, fraud, counterfeit)
- humbug (sham or hoax)
- consummate liar
- yarn spinner

Cheapskate
- miser
- niggard

Undesirable
- scamp
- blighter (one who blights; contemptible person)
- rotter
- churl
- rogue
- devil
- rapscallion (rascal)
- scapegrace (unprincipled rascal)
- scalawag
- scoundrel
- knave
- reprobate (depraved person)
- blackguard
- dregs of society
- scum of the earth
- villain
- ogre

Seducer
- gayblade
- profligate
- lecher
- libertine
- rounder
- debaucher
- philanderer
- wencher
- womanizer
- rake

Criminal
- desperado
- felon
- fiend
- gangster
- public enemy
- malefactor
- brute
- rowdy
- ruffian
- hoodlum
- hooligan
- goon
- thug
- bully
- rough
- scofflaw

Ungentlemanly Person
- churl
- cad
- bounder
- knave/lily livered knave

Animal Slurs
- black sheep
- louse
- rat
- cur
- mongrel
- whelp
- viper
- snake
- swine
- polecat (skunk)

Wanderer
truant
vagabond
derelict
undesirable
wretch
bad 'un
vagrant
ne'er do well
wastrel
idler

Woman
hellcat
vixen
she-devil
tigress
wildcat
siren
fury
Jezebel

Prostitute
soiled dove
lady of the night
red light lady
girl of the line (prostitute
    cribs lined alleys)
fallen woman
courtesan
wanton
painted lady
whore
trollop
strumpet
baggage
chippy
floozie
drab
harridan
frail sister

Good Fellow
paragon of virtue
capital fellow
good egg
decent sort
gentleman and a scholar
pillar of society
salt of the earth
true Christian
a man among men
a diamond in the rough
honest Abe

Good Woman
angel of light
person of the fair sex

Twelve: *Modern Rascals*

Present-day sneaks, crooks and villains earn different designations. Their schemes are just as wacky and their devious minds just as fertile. Just the names change. Now we label the less-than-law-abiding with names including:

tough	abuser	loser
hood	hate monger	bum
addict	racist	bar fly
creep	criminal	drunk
pornographer	offender	embezzler
perpetrator	jerk	

Though we have less in labels we certainly don't have fewer human foibles. Just several illicit escapades from the last few decades of Summit County history illustrate that fact.

Hanging Judge Gets the Rope

In the 1970s Summit County had two hanging judges. The first, a notorious alcoholic himself, cracked down on drunken drivers. He became the first to issue jail time for DUIs. The second, a woman, donned her judicial robes (over her exercise suit) and transformed into one tough magistrate. She struck fear into drunks behind the wheel. Amusingly, the male judge had earned a reputation as a hard drinker and late night celebrator in local bars. Many remembered his taking on-the-job nips—and naps. The woman judge wore red judicial robes when she was in a bad mood; then the guilty trembled. She herself was hauled in on a DUI but got off with little publicity and a hand slap. The male judge went undetained but did suffer the indignity of a bad fall off a bar stool.

Later the local justice system saw a female jail worker allegedly raid the jail-administered accounts of inmates to the tune of many thousands of dollars—the good guys robbing the bad guys! The case took so long to get to trial that witnesses forgot the details and the alleged embezzler got off.

Real Estate Heist

Realtors are almost as numerous today as miners were yesterday. And title companies probably match mining companies in numbers. In the early 1990s the president of a local title company concocted a legendary scheme to defraud Summit County government, the town of Frisco, the U.S. Forest Service and others of about $7 million.

Homestake Mining company of San Francisco, one of the participants in a multi-parcel real estate deal, expected to receive this same $7 million following the closing on several county land holdings. The property that today houses the County Commons, as well as other parcels in the deal, including a Forest Service land exchange, all changed hands in the transaction. The Homestead Mining Company's $7 million payment included a check for $1 million of county funds. The county treasurer, Larry Gilliland, hand-delivered the large check with the joking comment, "Don't spend it all in one place." The title company president paled slightly at the joke.

What he, the title company official, had done was to set up a bank account in the name of his phony venture, Homestake *Trading* Company, in Austria. He then scheduled the real estate closing for as late as possible on a Friday afternoon to buy himself time. When the closing finished and the $7 million for Homestake in San Francisco was in his hand, the title man used an arrangement set up earlier for an international funds transfer by wire to his account in Austria. The money would pass through banks in Denver and New York.

The would-be swindler then drove to Denver and boarded a flight to Austria, sure that the weekend would provide the necessary cloak for his plot. Homestake Mining Company staff in San Francisco made telephone calls when their expected funds wire failed to arrive but closed offices in earlier time zones frustrated their efforts.

However, an alert staffer in the local title company office saw small signs that made her uneasy. She telephoned Denver bank personnel but found the funds were already forwarded to New York. Finally she got a banker in New York, who working frantically after hours, scrambled to investigate. In a move unusual with international wire transfers, the bank managed to get the payment stopped.

When the nearly-*nouveau-riche* Coloradoan appeared at the Austrian bank Monday morning, he inquired pleasantly, "Is my money here yet?" "No," was the equally pleasant answer. But the FBI is here and they're looking for *you*!"

Local officers later discovered information on aliases and false identification documents, plus several heavy duty weapons in a locked credenza in the title president's office.

Stories like this one add pepper to the miscreant stew of the Summit County criminal sub-culture. A second "Rascals" book could be written on the current capers of cheats, embezzlers and frauds, not to mention loose-livers and mischief-makers. Plus shysters and cads.

People are already offering to buy their way out of this second book.

INDEX

PHOTO CREDITS

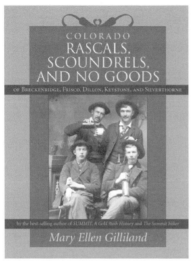

Order a Copy of *RASCALS* for a Friend

Give this collection of characters from Colorado mine camp history to another book lover. Readers love the misdeeds and misadventures of this book's disreputable 1800s crew.

Please see Order Blank on last page.

Ghost towns • Ute Indians • stagecoaching • narrow-gauge railways • mine camps • gold and silver saga • jeep tour guides • mineral towns

Find it all in *SUMMIT, A Gold Rush History of Summit County, Colorado*. Lively, well-written 348-page history with over 100 antique photographs.

Please see Order Blank on last page

50 historic hiking trails take you to alpine lakes and waterfalls, ghost camps, historic high passes and wildflower meadows.

The New Summit Hiker & Ski Touring Guide, newly revised in its seventh edition also provides 22 scenic ski and snowshoe trails and Special Hikes for Kids.

Please see Order Blank on last page.

Explore the unspoiled Holy Cross and Eagles Nest wilderness areas with *The Vail Hiker & Ski Touring Guide*. 50 trails for every level from a "Hikes for Kids" section to adventures for mountaineers.

USGS topo maps an detailed directions.

Best-selling book in Vail stores!

Please see order blank on last page.

Alpenrose
Press

ORDER BLANK

Name_____

Address_____

City _____State _____Zip _____

Quantity	Title	Tax	Price
_____	Rascals, Scoundrels & No-Goods		19.95
	Colo. only Tax		1.13
_____	SUMMIT		22.95
	Colo. only tax		1.30
_____	Breckenridge!		4.95
	Colo. only tax		.28
_____	The New Summit Hiker		16.95
	Colo. only tax		.96
_____	The Vail Hiker		17.95
	Colo. only tax		1.00

Postage & Handling @ $3 each book   _____
(3 or more books – Free Postage!)

Total Enclosed   _____

Check or Money Order Only
Send to: Alpenrose Press, Box 499, Silverthorne, CO 80498

Request Author Autograph!
  Please autography my copy to: (Name)_____